Carrying on in Key Stage 1

Providing continuity in purposeful play and exploration

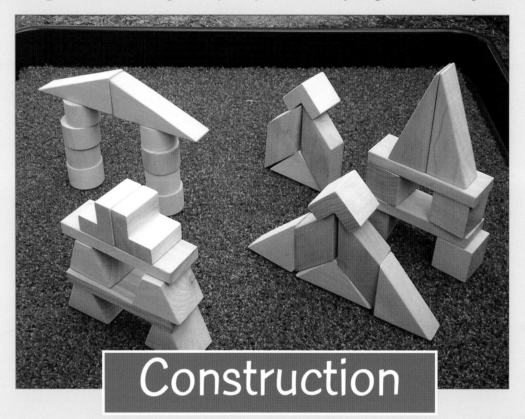

Construction

Ros Bayley, Lynn Broadbent, Sally Featherstone

Reprinted 2009
Published 2008 by A&C Black Publishers Limited
36 Soho Square, London W1D 3QY
www.acblack.com

ISBN 978-1-906029-12-8

First published 2008 by Featherstone Education Limited

Text © Ros Bayley, Lyn Broadbent, Sally Featherstone 2008
Illustrations © Kerry Ingham 2008
Photographs © Lynn Broadbent, Ros Bayley,
Sally Featherstone, Sarah Featherstone 2008

A CIP record for this publication is available from the British Library.

Printed in Malta by Gutenberg Press Ltd

This book is produced using paper that is made from wood grown in
managed, sustainable forests. It is natural, renewable and recyclable.
The logging and manufacturing processes conform to the environmental
regulations of the country of origin.

To see our full range of titles

visit www.acblack.com

Contents

Introduction

This series of books is intended to support the continuing growth and development of independent learning and practical activities, which are key features of the Early Years Foundation Stage.

Children in Key Stage One need and deserve the chance to build on the best of practice in the Early Years Foundation Stage, which carefully balances adult directed tasks with learning that children initiate and develop themselves, often in the company of responsive adults. These activities, which include sand and water play, construction, role play, independent mark making and writing, creative work, dance and movement, and outdoor play, are some of the activities children value most and miss most in Years One and Two.

Parent: 'What's it like in Year 1?'

Child: 'It's OK, but there's hundreds of learning and we don't go outside much.'

This quote from a Year 1 boy echoes the feelings of many children who need to continue the learning styles and situations offered in Reception classes. However, many teachers in Key Stage One feel intense pressure to concentrate on activities that require recording and increasing levels of direction by adults. Why is this, and is it right for teachers to feel so pressured?

One thing we know from research is that practical activity and independent learning are essential for brain growth and reinforcement of growing abilities throughout childhood, at least till the onset of puberty, and for many children this is a lifelong need. We also know that the embedding of learning and the transformation of this into real understanding takes time and practice. Skills need to be reinforced by revisiting them in many different contexts in child initiated learning, and practical challenges, and practical tasks in real life situations will be far more effective than rote learning, worksheets or adult direction.

'I hear and I forget,

I see and I remember,

I do and I understand.'

Ancient Chinese Proverb

It is also clear from brain research that many boys (and some girls) are just not ready by the end of Reception to embark on a formal curriculum which involves a lot of sitting down, listening and writing. Their bodies and their brains still need action, challenge and freedom to explore materials and resources in freedom.

But this does not mean that challenge should be absent from such activity! The brain feeds on challenge and novelty, so teachers and other adults working in Key Stage One need to structure the experiences, so they build on existing skills and previous activities, while presenting new opportunities to explore familiar materials in new and exciting ways. Such challenges and activities can:

EVERY
CHILD MATTERS
The five outcomes:
Enjoy and achieve
Stay safe
Be healthy
Make a positive contribution
Achieve economic
well-being

- be led by the Programme of Study for Key Stage One;
- focus on thinking skills and personal capabilities;
- relate to real world situations and stimuli;
- help children to achieve the five outcomes for Every Child Matters.

In **Carrying on in Key Stage 1**, we aim to give you the rationale, the process and the confidence to continue a practical, child centred curriculum which also helps you as teachers to recognise the requirements of the statutory curriculum for Key Stage One. Each book in the series follows the same format, and addresses objectives from many areas of the National Curriculum. Of course, when children work on practical challenges, curriculum elements become intertwined, and many will be going on simultaneously.

The role of the adult

Of course, even during child initiated learning, the role of the adult is crucial. Sensitive adults play many roles as they support, challenge and engage the children in their care. High quality teaching is not easy! If teachers want to expand experiences and enhance learning, they need to be able to stand back, to work alongside, <u>and</u> extend or scaffold the children's learning by offering provocations and challenges to their thinking and activity. The diagram below attempts to describe this complex task, and the way that adults move around the elements in the circle of learning. For ease of reading we have described the elements in the following way, and each double page spread covers all three of the vital roles adults play.

Recognising and building on the practical activities which children have experienced before

This element of the process is vital in scaffolding children's learning so it makes sense to them. Your knowledge of the Foundation Stage curriculum and the way it is organised will be vital in knowing where to start. Teachers and other adults should have first hand knowledge of both the resources and the activities which have been available and how they have been offered in both child initiated and adult led activities. This knowledge should be gained by visiting the Reception classes in action, and by talking to adults and children as they work. Looking at Reception planning will also help.

Understanding the range of adult roles, and the effect different roles have on children's learning

Responsive adults react in different ways to what they see and hear during the day. This knowledge will influence the way they plan for further experiences which meet emerging needs and build on individual interests. The diagram illustrates the complex and interlinking ways in which adults interact with children's learning. Observing, co-playing and extending learning often happen simultaneously, flexibly and sometime unconsciously. It is only when we reflect on our work with children that we realise what a complex and skilled activity is going on.

Offering challenges and provocations

As the adults collect information about the learning, they begin to see how they can help children to extend and scaffold their thinking and learning. The adults offer challenges or provocations which act like grit in an oyster, provoking the children to produce responses and think in new ways about what they know and can do.

Linking the learning with the skills and content of the curriculum

As the children grapple with new concepts and skills, adults can make direct links with curriculum intentions and content. These links can be mapped out across the range of knowledge, skills and understanding contained in the curriculum guidance for Key Stage One. It is also possible to map the development of thinking skills, personal capabilities and concepts which link the taught curriculum with the real world.

The adult as extender of learning
discusses ideas
shares thinking
makes new possibilities evident
instigates new opportunities for learning
extends and builds on learning and interests
supports children in making links in learning
models new skills and techniques

The adult as co-player
shares responsibility with the child
offers suggestions
asks open questions
responds sensitively
models and imitates
plays alongside

The adult as observer
listens attentively
observes carefully
records professionally
interprets skilfully

Looking for the learning

As children plan, explore, invent, extend, construct, discuss, question and predict in the rich experiences planned and offered, they will communicate what they are learning through speech and actions, as well as through the outcomes of activities. Assessment for learning involves adults and children in discussing and analysing what they discover. Reflecting on learning, through discussion with other children and adults, is a key factor in securing skills and abilities, fixing and 'hard wiring' the learning in each child's brain. And, of course, teachers and other adults need to recognise, confirm and record children's achievements, both for the self esteem this brings to the children and to fulfil their own duties as educators.

You could find out what children already know and have experienced by:

* talking to them as individuals and in small groups;

* talking to parents and other adults who know them well (teaching assistants are often wonderful sources of information about individual children);

* visiting the Reception classes and looking at spaces, storage and access to resources, including the use of these out of doors;

* providing free access to materials and equipment and watching how children use them when you are not giving any guidance;

* talking as a group or class about what children already know about the materials and those they particularly enjoy using.

Using the curriculum grid to observe, to recognise learning and celebrate achievement

At the end of each section you will find a curriculum grid which covers the whole Programme of Study for Key Stage 1. This is a 'shorthand version' of the full grid included at the end of the book on pages 69-74. A black and white photocopiable version of the grid appears on page 8, so you can make your own copies for planning and particularly for recording observations.

We suggest that as the children work on the provocations and other challenges in this book, adults (teachers and teaching assistants) can use the grid to observe groups of children and record the areas of the curriculum they are covering in their work. The grids can also be used to record what children say and describe in plenary sessions and other discussions.

These observations will enable you to recognise the learning that happens as children explore the materials and engage with the challenging questions you ask and the problems you pose. And of course, as you observe, you will begin to see what needs to happen next; identifying the next steps in learning! This logical and vital stage in the process may identify:

* some children who will be ready for more of the same activity;

* some who need to repeat and reinforce previous stages;

* some who need to relate skills to new contexts, the same activity or skill practiced in a new place or situation;

* some who will want to extend or sustain the current activity in time, space or detail;

* others who will wish to record their work in photos, drawings, models, stories, video etc.

Critical and Thinking Skills

The grid also identifies the key skills which children need for thinking about and evaluating their work. Many schools now observe and evaluate how well these skills are developing when children work on challenging projects and investigations.

Taking it further

Offering extension activities is a way of scaffolding children's learning, taking the known into the unknown, the familiar into the new, the secure into the challenging. It is the role of the adult to turn their knowledge of the children into worthwhile, long term lines of enquiry and development which will become self-sustaining and last throughout life.

At the end of each section in the book you will find a selection of useful resources, links and other information to help you bring construction to life. You could use these resources by encouraging individuals and groups:

* to **use the Internet** to find images and information;

* to **use ICT equipment** such as cameras, tape recorders, video and dictaphones to record their explorations and experiments;

* to **explore information books** in libraries and other places at home and at school;

* to **make contact by email** and letter with experts, craftsmen, artists, manufacturers, suppliers and other contacts;

* to **make books, films, PowerPoint presentations;**

* to **record their work** in photographs and other media;

* to **respond to** photographs, video, exhibitions and other creative stimuli;

* to **look at the built and natural environment** with curiosity, interest and creativity;

* to **become involved in preserving the natural world**, develop environmental awareness and support recycling;

* to **look at the world of work** and extend their ideas of what they might become and how they might live their lives;

* to **develop a sense of economic awareness** and the world of work in its widest sense;

* to **feel a sense of community** and to explore how they might make a contribution to the school and wider communities in which they live;

* to **work together and develop the ability to think, reason and solve problems** in their learning.

We recommend that younger children should always work with an adult when accessing search engines and Internet sites.

The suggested resources include websites, books, contacts and addresses. There are also some photographs which may inspire young learners as they work on the provocations and challenges suggested.

We hope you will find the ideas in this book useful in stimulating your work with children in Year 1 and Year 2. The ideas, photos and provocations we have included are only a start to your thinking and exploring together. Of course you and the children will have many more as you start to expand the work they do in these practical areas, providing a rich curriculum base using familiar and well loved materials.

Ros Bayley, Lynn Broadbent, Sally Featherstone; 2007

Observation of _____ (the activity and resources)

Literacy

Lit 1 speak	Lit 2 listen	Lit 3 group	Lit 4 drama	Lit 5 word	Lit 6 spell	Lit 7 text1	Lit 8 text2	Lit 9 text3	Lit10 text4	Lit11 sentence	Lit12 presentation
1.1	2.1	3.1	4.1	5.1	6.1	7.1	8.1	9.1	10.1	11.1	12.1
1.2	2.2	3.2	4.2	5.2	6.2	7.2	8.2	9.2	10.2	11.2	12.2

Numeracy

Num 1 U&A	Num 2 count	Num 3 number	Num 4 calculate	Num 5 shape	Num 6 measure	Num 7 data
1.1	2.1	3.1	4.1	5.1	6.1	7.1
1.2	2.2	3.2	4.2	5.2	6.2	7.2

Date _____

Names _____

Science

SC1 Enquiry			SC2 Life processes					SC3 Materials		SC4 Phys processes		
Sc1.1	Sc1.2	Sc1.3	Sc2.1	Sc2.2	Sc2.3	Sc2.4	Sc2.5	Sc3.1	Sc3.2	Sc4.1	Sc4.2	Sc4.3
1.1a	1.2a	1.3a	2.1a	2.2a	2.3a	2.4a	2.5a	3.1a	3.2a	4.1a	4.2a	4.3a
1.1b	1.2b	1.3b	2.1b	2.2b	2.3b	2.4b	2.5b	3.1b	3.2b	4.1b	4.2b	4.3b
1.1c	1.2c	1.3c	2.1c	2.2c	2.3c		2.5c	3.1c		4.1c	4.2c	4.3c
1.1d				2.2d				3.1d				4.3d
				2.2e								
				2.2f								
				2.2g								

ICT

ICT 1 finding out		ICT 2 ideas	ICT 3 reviewing	ICT 4 breadth
1.1a	1.2a	2a	3a	4a
1.1b	1.2b	2b	3b	4b
1.1c	1.2c	2c	3c	4c
	1.2d			

PE

PE1 devel skills	PE2 apply skills	PE3 evaluate	PE4 fitness	PE5 breadth
1a	2a	3a	4a	5a dance
1b	2b	3b	4b	5b games
	2c	3c		5c gym

Art & Design

A&D1 ideas	A&D2 making	A&D3 evaluating	A&D4 materials	A&D5 breadth
1a	2a	3a	4a	5a
1b	2b	3b	4b	5b
	2c		4c	5c
				5d

History

H1 chronology	H2 events, people	H3 interpret	H4 enquire	H5 org & comm	H6 breadth
1a	2a	3a	4a	5a	6a
1b	2b		4b		6b
					6c
					6d

Geography

G1.1 & G1.2 enquiry		G2 places	G3 processes	G4 environment	G5 breadth
1.1a	1.2a	2a	3a	4a	5a
1.1b	1.2b	2b	3b	4b	5b
1.1c	1.2c	2c			5c
1.1d	1.2d	2d			5d
		2e			

PHSE & C

PSHEC1 conf & resp	PSHEC2 citizenship	PSHEC3 health	PSHEC4 relationships
1a	2a	3a	4a
1b	2b	3b	4b
1c	2c	3c	4c
1d	2d	3d	4d
1e	2e	3e	4e
	2f	3f	
	2g	3g	
	2h		

D&T

D&T 1 developing	D&T 2 tool use	D&T 3 evaluating	D&T 4 materials	D&T 5 breadth
1a	2a	3a	4a	5a
1b	2b	3b	4b	5b
1c	2c			5c
1d	2d			
1e	2e			

Music

M1 performing	M2 composing	M3 appraising	M4 listening	M5 breadth
1a	2a	3a	4a	5a
1b	2b	3b	4b	5b
1c			4c	5c
				5d

Critical Skills	Thinking Skills
problem solving	observing
decision making	classifying
critical thinking	prediction
creative thinking	making inferences
communication	problem solving
organisation	drawing conclusions
management	
leadership	

Notes on how to take the learning forward:

Key to KS1 PoS on Pages 69-74

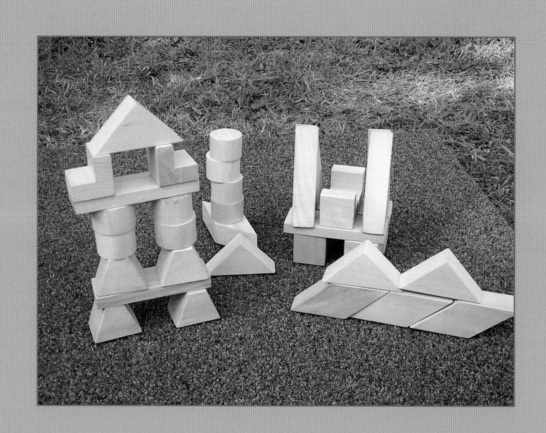

Wooden bricks

Wooden bricks

Previous experience in the Foundation Stage

Children may have had previous experience with wooden bricks in child initiated learning and adult led activities such as:

* free play indoors and out of doors;
* combined with small world (to make habitats, buildings, roadways, bridges, tunnels);
* carried to and included in other provision (eg sand, role play, superhero play, small world);
* to represent other objects in role play (money, food, rocks, people);
* to count, pattern, order, recognise shapes;
* to explore spatial relationships in 3D;
* in classification activities (shape, size etc);
* to make constructions such as bridges and buildings they have seen in real life or pictures.

Pause for thought

In the early stages of working with these materials it is crucial to continue to observe the children. Only by doing this can you set developmentally appropriate challenges and provocations. The ideas listed here are offered as suggestions; the most exciting challenges will arise from children's own interests and motivations, which will only become apparent as you spend time with them, watching and joining them in their play. As you do this, you will be moving between the three interconnecting roles of observer, co-player, extender described below, and will be able to decide what you need to do next to take the learning forward.

The responsive adult (see page 5)

In three interconnecting roles, the responsive adult will be:

* observing
* listening
* interpreting

observer

* **modelling**
* **playing alongside**
* **offering suggestions**
* **responding sensitively**
* **initiating with care!**

co-player

* discussing ideas
* sharing thinking
* modelling new skills
* asking open questions
* being an informed extender
* instigating ideas & thoughts
* supporting children as they make links in learning
* making possibilities evident
* introducing new ideas and resources
* offering challenges and provocations

extender

Offering challenges and provocations - some ideas:

? What is the highest building/the longest building you can make?

? Can you make a building that uses all the bricks?

? Which are the best bricks for making towers? tunnels? slopes?

? Could you make a building like this? or like this? (responding to paintings of buildings, bridges and other structures)

? How did they make a building like this? (responding to photos of buildings)

? Who might live here? (looking at unusual buildings)

? What sort of house would this person live in? (responding to photos of people or characters)

? Could you make a home for this toy? Or this small world character?

? How do builders make arches? Towers? Windows in brick buildings?

? Can you make a building with just the triangular bricks, or just the cylinders?

? Could you use the bricks to make a sculpture like the Iron Man or the Angel of the North?

? Can you build a bridge strong enough to carry a toy car? a bike? or a person?

? Can you make a hollow building, with room inside for toy cars or people?

? Find a picture of a building in a book. Can you make the building with bricks?

? Make a building using every brick in your collection. How many bricks did you use in your building? Did you use them all?

Ready for more?

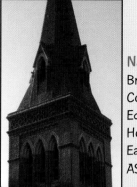

- Can you make a completely symmetrical building?
- Could you make a castle, then make a film with characters?
- Planning and creating a sustained project (for example, building a large structure and photographing it over time).
- Design and make a hollow building with no doors or windows.
- Make a construction in the style of...; (suggest and look at building styles which suit the shapes and proportions of the bricks the children are using, try Canary Wharf, St Paul's Cathedral, Buckingham Palace, Windsor Castle, Tower Bridge)
- Plan and draw a labelled diagram of a building; build it according to your plan.
- With two friends, use all the bricks to build a structure.
- Devise your own criteria for sorting the bricks into sets.
- Find a big space. Now make a structure that is only one brick high, but uses all the bricks in the set. Try to fit the bricks together without leaving spaces. What shape is your building? Did you use all the bricks?

Materials, equipment suppliers, websites, books and other references

Natural wooden and painted wooden brick sets from:
Brio: www.brio.co.uk
Community Playthings: www.communityplaythings.co.uk
Eduzone: www.eduzone.co.uk
Hope: www.hope-education.co.uk
Early Learning Centre: www.elc.co.uk
ASCO: www.ascoeducational.co.uk

For images of buildings try Google Images. Just enter the name or type of the building you want to see ('castle' 'Tower of London' 'Bridge' 'mosque' 'town hall' etc).

Try The Building Centre www.buildingcentre.org.uk go to 'links/education' and find the school of architecture nearest to you. they might be interested in working with the children on a project!

Some suitable books for younger readers include:
Joe and the Skyscraper; Deitrich Neumann; Prestel Verlag
Homes and Houses; Usborne
Mosque, Synagogue, Sikh Temple and other places of worship; A&C Black
Building; Philip Wilkinson; DK Eyewitness
Castle; Nicholas Harris; Chrysalis Children's Books
Houses and Homes; Claire Llewellyn; Evans Brothers
Stephen Biesty's Castles; Stephen Biesty; Hodder

Some picture books for inspiration:
Richard Rogers: Complete works; Phaidon Press
Frank O Gehry: Complete Works; Kurt Foster; Electa Architecture
Zaha Hadid: 30 Years of Architecture; Joseph Giovannini; Guggenheim Museum Publications

Curriculum coverage grid overleaf

Potential NC KS1 Curriculum Coverage through the provocations suggested for wooden bricks.

Literacy

	Lit 1 speak	Lit 2 listen	Lit 3 group	Lit 4 drama	Lit 5 word	Lit 6 spell	Lit 7 text1	Lit 8 text2	Lit 9 text3	Lit10 text4	Lit11 sentence	Lit12 presentation
Literacy	1.1	2.1	3.1	4.1	5.1	6.1	7.1	8.1	9.1	10.1	11.1	12.1
	1.2	2.2	3.2	4.2	5.2	6.2	7.2	8.2	9.2	10.2	11.2	12.2

Numeracy

	Num 1 U&A	Num 2 count	Num 3 number	Num 4 calculate	Num 5 shape	Num 6 measure	Num 7 data
Numeracy	1.1	2.1	3.1	4.1	5.1	6.1	7.1
	1.2	2.2	3.2	4.2	5.2	6.2	7.2

This chart has been included to help you track the objectives from the **Key Stage 1 curriculum**, which the children may cover as they work on projects, challenges and provocations using **wooden bricks**.

A full version of the KS1 PoS objectives appears on Pages 69-74, a photocopiable version is included on Page 8.

Science

	SC1 Enquiry			SC2 Life processes					SC3 Materials		SC4 Phys processes		
	Sc1.1	Sc1.2	Sc1.3	Sc2.1	Sc2.2	Sc2.3	Sc2.4	Sc2.5	Sc3.1	Sc3.2	Sc4.1	Sc4.2	Sc4.3
Science	1.1a	1.2a	1.3a	2.1a	2.2a	2.3a	2.4a	2.5a	3.1a	3.2a	4.1a	4.2a	4.3a
	1.1b	1.2b	1.3b	2.1b	2.2b	2.3b	2.4b	2.5b	3.1b	3.2b	4.1b	4.2b	4.3b
	1.1c	1.2c	1.3c	2.1c	2.2c	2.3c		2.5c	3.1c		4.1c	4.2c	4.3c
	1.1d				2.2d				3.1d				4.3d
					2.2e								
					2.2f								
					2.2g								

ICT

	ICT 1 finding out		ICT 2 ideas	ICT 3 reviewing	ICT 4 breadth
ICT	1.1a	1.2a	2a	3a	4a
	1.1b	1.2b	2b	3b	4b
	1.1c	1.2c	2c	3c	4c
		1.2d			

D&T

	D&T 1 developing	D&T 2 tool use	D&T 3 evaluating	D&T 4 materials	D&T 5 breadth
D&T	1a	2a	3a	4a	5a
	1b	2b	3b	4b	5b
	1c	2c			5c
	1d	2d			
	1e	2e			

History

	H1 chronology	H2 events, people	H3 interpret	H4 enquire	H5 org & comm	H6 breadth
History	1a	2a	3a	4a	5a	6a
	1b	2b		4b		6b
						6c
						6d

Geography

	G1.1 & G1.2 enquiry		G2 places	G3 processes	G4 environment	G5 breadth
Geography	1.1a	1.2a	2a	3a	4a	5a
	1.1b	1.2b	2b	3b	4b	5b
	1.1c	1.2c	2c			5c
	1.1d	1.2d	2d			5d
			2e			

Music

	M1 performing	M2 composing	M3 appraising	M4 listening	M5 breadth
Music	1a	2a	3a	4a	5a
	1b	2b	3b	4b	5b
	1c			4c	5c
					5d

PSHE & C

	PSHEC1 conf & resp	PSHEC2 citizenship	PSHEC3 health	PSHEC4 relationships
PHSE & C	1a	2a	3a	4a
	1b	2b	3b	4b
	1c	2c	3c	4c
	1d	2d	3d	4d
	1e	2e	3e	4e
		2f	3f	
		2g	3g	
		2h		

Art & Design

	A&D1 ideas	A&D2 making	A&D3 evaluating	A&D4 materials	A&D5 breadth
Art & Design	1a	2a	3a	4a	5a
	1b	2b	3b	4b	5b
		2c		4c	5c
					5d

PE

	PE1 devel skills	PE2 apply skills	PE3 evaluate	PE4 fitness	PE5 breadth
PE	1a	2a	3a	4a	5a dance
	1b	2b	3b	4b	5b games
		2c	3c		5c gym

Critical skills	Thinking Skills
problem solving	observing
decision making	classifying
critical thinking	prediction
creative thinking	making inferences
communication	problem solving
organisation	drawing conclusions
management	
leadership	

Straws and connecting rods

Straws and connecting rods

Previous experience in the Foundation Stage

These materials consist of rods and straws which are linked by joining units. Children may have had previous experience with them in child initiated learning and adult led activities such as:

* free play indoors and out of doors;
* combined with small world (shelters, vehicles and furniture);
* to represent other objects in role play (wheels, umbrellas, rockets, insects);
* the lightness of some kits enables children to make child sized structures to enter and explore;
* to explore spatial relationships in 3D;
* to make hats, helmets and crowns;
* larger kits such as Quadro enable children to make constructions such as cars, trolleys and trucks to ride on.

Pause for thought

In the early stages of working with these materials it is crucial to continue to observe the children. Only by doing this can you set developmentally appropriate challenges and provocations. The ideas listed here are offered as suggestions; the most exciting challenges will arise from children's own interests and motivations, which will only become apparent as you spend time with them, watching and joining them in their play. As you do this, you will be moving between the three interconnecting roles of observer, co-player, extender described below, and will be able to decide what you need to do next to take the learning forward.

The responsive adult (see page 5)

In three interconnecting roles, the responsive adult will be:

observer

* observing
* listening
* interpreting

co-player

* **modelling**
* **playing alongside**
* **offering suggestions**
* **responding sensitively**
* **initiating with care!**

extender

* discussing ideas
* sharing thinking
* modelling new skills
* asking open questions
* being an informed extender
* instigating ideas & thoughts
* supporting children as they make links in learning
* making possibilities evident
* introducing new ideas and resources
* offering challenges and provocations

Offering challenges and provocations - some ideas:

? Make a tall crane. What it can lift?
? Make a hanging mobile for the garden.
? Make some scaffolding for a brick building.
? Can you make a bridge that will carry a toy car?
? Can you use the kit to make some furniture for soft toys or dolls?
? Can you make a vehicle for a farm, for mountain climbing, for driving on the moon?
? Find a fantasy character and make a fantasy home for them. You can add light fabric or paper for walls if you like.
? Google some of the suggested words and print some of the images as inspiration. Choose ones that resemble the particular kits you have in your room.
? Look up The Eden Project and work together on making domes and other buildings with linking straws and rods.
? Visit a street market, or look at some pictures of market stalls. Try making market stalls with the materials, use card for the table tops and fabric or paper for the roofs and sides.
? Look at some electricity pylons or telegraph poles. Try making some with kits and string.
? Design and make a windmill or water mill. Test the wheel with water or go outside to test it in the wind. What happens?
? Can you make a game with the straws? Look up Pick a Stick or Spillikins on Google to help you.

Ready for more?

- Can you make a hanging wind mobile for the garden? Make it so it spins in the wind.
- Build a tall building with wooden bricks. Now make scaffolding in stages and take photos as the scaffolding goes up the building.
- Find a new way to join straws. Get some drinking straws and find a way to join them. Think, look and try lots of different ways. Which is best? Have you invented a new toy?
- Use the pieces to make a greenhouse. Cover the greenhouse with plastic or cling film. Could you use it to grow seeds in? Try! You could use mustard and cress seeds or beans to grow for your experiment.
- Look up 'bridge' or 'crane' on Google. Find a bridge that would be easy to copy with straws, KNex or Mobilo. Make your own bridge.
- Use the straws to make a structure that can carry a toy vehicle of a small character over a gap between two tables or two piles of bricks. What is the best way to do this?
- Use straws to make spinners that will spin in the wind outside. Find a way to fix them to a fence or wall.

Materials, equipment suppliers, websites, books and other references

Suppliers of straws and other straw construction materials:
ASCO: www.ascoeducational.co.uk For Link Kits (big size), Mobilo, Maxi-Kit Tech.
Galt products: www.mailorderexpress.com for Connecta-straws and Straw Art Kit.
Construction Toys: www.constructiontoys.com for Erector & Querceti Marble Run.
Artastik: www.artastic.co.uk for paper Artstraws and books on how to use them.

For useful images of buildings and other structures, try **Google Images**. Just enter the name or type of building you want to see ('straw structures' 'construct straws' 'crane' 'millenium wheel' 'suspension bridge' 'longest bridge' 'thatch' 'scaffolding' 'greenhouses' 'pylons' etc).

Try the Guild of Straw Craftsmen www.strawcraftmen.co.uk and click on 'straw related articles' for 'thatch' 'cards' 'decorations'. **Google** 'wikipedia' then look for 'longest bridge' or 'Eden' for lots of information and pictures.

Some suitable **books** for younger readers include:
Crane; DK Machines at Work
A Day at the Eden Project; C Petty; Collins Big Cat
Eden; Tim Smit; Corgi
The Book of Wheat Weaving & Straw Crafts; Owens Celli; Lark Books
Bridges, and **Skyscrapers**; both by CA Johmann; Kaleidoscope
and some **picture books** for inspiration:
The Brooklyn Bridge; Elizabeth Mann; Miyako Press
The Longest Bridge; Darv Johnson; Kidhaven Architecture
Brunel, the man who Built the World; Steven Brindle; Phoenix
30000 Years of Defying Nature; DJ Brown; Mitchell Beazley

Curriculum coverage grid overleaf

Potential NC KS1 Curriculum Coverage through the provocations suggested for straws and rods

Literacy

	Lit 1 speak	Lit 2 listen	Lit 3 group	Lit 4 drama	Lit 5 word	Lit 6 spell	Lit 7 text1	Lit 8 text2	Lit 9 text3	Lit10 text4	Lit11 sentence	Lit12 presentation
Literacy	1.1	2.1	3.1	4.1	5.1	6.1	7.1	8.1	9.1	10.1	11.1	12.1
	1.2	2.2	3.2	4.2	5.2	6.2	7.2	8.2	9.2	10.2	11.2	12.2

Numeracy

	Num 1 U&A	Num 2 count	Num 3 number	Num 4 calculate	Num 5 shape	Num 6 measure	Num 7 data
Numeracy	1.1	2.1	3.1	4.1	5.1	6.1	7.1
	1.2	2.2	3.2	4.2	5.2	6.2	7.2

This chart has been included to help you track the objectives from the **Key Stage 1 curriculum**, which the children may cover as they work on projects, challenges and provocations using **straws and KNex**.

A full version of the KS1 PoS objectives appears on Pages 69-74, a photocopiable version is included on Page 8.

Science

	SC1 Enquiry			SC2 Life processes					SC3 Materials		SC4 Phys processes		
	Sc1.1	Sc1.2	Sc1.3	Sc2.1	Sc2.2	Sc2.3	Sc2.4	Sc2.5	Sc3.1	Sc3.2	Sc4.1	Sc4.2	Sc4.3
Science	1.1a	1.2a	1.3a	2.1a	2.2a	2.3a	2.4a	2.5a	3.1a	3.2a	4.1a	4.2a	4.3a
	1.1b	1.2b	1.3b	2.1b	2.2b	2.3b	2.4b	2.5b	3.1b	3.2b	4.1b	4.2b	4.3b
	1.1c	1.2c	1.3c	2.1c	2.2c	2.3c		2.5c	3.1c		4.1c	4.2c	4.3c
	1.1d				2.2d				3.1d				4.3d
					2.2e								
					2.2f								
					2.2g								

ICT

	ICT 1 finding out		ICT 2 ideas	ICT 3 reviewing	ICT 4 breadth
ICT	1.1a	1.2a	2a	3a	4a
	1.1b	1.2b	2b	3b	4b
	1.1c	1.2c	2c	3c	4c
		1.2d			

D&T

	D&T 1 developing	D&T 2 tool use	D&T 3 evaluating	D&T 4 materials	D&T 5 breadth
D&T	1a	2a	3a	4a	5a
	1b	2b	3b	4b	5b
	1c	2c			5c
	1d	2d			
	1e	2e			

History

	H1 chronology	H2 events, people	H3 interpret	H4 enquire	H5 org & comm	H6 breadth
History	1a	2a	3a	4a	5a	6a
	1b	2b		4b		6b
						6c
						6d

Geography

	G1.1 & G1.2 enquiry		G2 places	G3 processes	G4 environment	G5 breadth
Geography	1.1a	1.2a	2a	3a	4a	5a
	1.1b	1.2b	2b	3b	4b	5b
	1.1c	1.2c	2c			5c
	1.1d	1.2d	2d			5d
			2e			

Music

	M1 performing	M2 composing	M3 appraising	M4 listening	M5 breadth
Music	1a	2a	3a	4a	5a
	1b	2b	3b	4b	5b
	1c			4c	5c
					5d

PHSE & C

	PSHEC1 conf & resp	PSHEC2 citizenship	PSHEC3 health	PSHEC4 relationships
PHSE & C	1a	2a	3a	4a
	1b	2b	3b	4b
	1c	2c	3c	4c
	1d	2d	3d	4d
	1e	2e	3e	4e
		2f	3f	
		2g	3g	
		2h		

Art & Design

	A&D1 ideas	A&D2 making	A&D3 evaluating	A&D4 materials	A&D5 breadth
Art & Design	1a	2a	3a	4a	5a
	1b	2b	3b	4b	5b
		2c		4c	5c
					5d

PE

	PE1 devel skills	PE2 apply skills	PE3 evaluate	PE4 fitness	PE5 breadth
PE	1a	2a	3a	4a	5a dance
	1b	2b	3b	4b	5b games
		2c	3c		5c gym

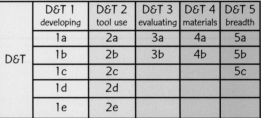

Critical skills	Thinking Skills
problem solving	observing
decision making	classifying
critical thinking	prediction
creative thinking	making inferences
communication	problem solving
organisation	drawing conclusions
management	
leadership	

Construction sets

Construction sets

Previous experience in the Foundation Stage

Most early construction sets (such as Lego, Stickle Bricks, Mobilo) consist of standard shapes in several sizes which clip together to form structures. These are standard equipment in all Foundation rooms. Children will have used them:

* in free play to make structures, habitats etc;
* with small world people or matching people provided with the kits;
* to experiment with shape, size and pattern in two and three dimensions;
* to explore making steady structures;
* in collaborative activities with other children, making structures and objects which relate to each other - cars for a roadway, people for a town, planes or space rockets, then using these in imaginative play.

Pause for thought

In the early stages of working with these materials it is crucial to continue to observe the children. Only by doing this can you set developmentally appropriate challenges and provocations. The ideas listed here are offered as suggestions; the most exciting challenges will arise from children's own interests and motivations, which will only become apparent as you spend time with them, watching and joining them in their play. As you do this, you will be moving between the three interconnecting roles of observer, co-player, extender described below, and will be able to decide what you need to do next to take the learning forward.

The responsive adult (see page 5)

In three interconnecting roles, the responsive adult will be:

observer

* observing
* listening
* interpreting

co-player

* **modelling**
* **playing alongside**
* **offering suggestions**
* **responding sensitively**
* **initiating with care!**

extender

* discussing ideas
* sharing thinking
* modelling new skills
* asking open questions
* being an informed extender
* instigating ideas & thoughts
* supporting children as they make links in learning
* making possibilities evident
* introducing new ideas and resources
* offering challenges and provocations

Offering challenges and provocations - some ideas:

Children are less likely to have used construction sets in adult directed activities. They may need practice in accepting and carrying out challenges presented by adults - you may need to introduce this gradually and sit with the children as they work to encourage them to stay on task!

? Can you build a structure using pieces of all the same colour?

? Can you make a wheeled vehicle for a fantasy character?

? Which is the best way to build a firm wall? Try different ways and take photos of your experiments. Look at some walls outside and at home. How are they made strong?

? Can you make a structure taller than you?

? Make the longest wheeled structure you can. Measure it.

? Explore how you can make curved shapes with rectangular or square bricks.

? Use the internet to find the Lego site or put 'Lego model' in Google. Have a go at copying some of the models you find. Photograph your best ones and send them to the Lego magazine.

? Sort out all the unusual bricks in the set. What can you make with these?

? Make a structure with a roof. What is the best way to make a roof that will stay on?

? Make a low, flat building that covers as much floor space as possible. Take some photos of your best buildings.

Ready for more?

- Ask a friend to pick a number from 1 to 100. Make a structure or vehicle using exactly that number of pieces. Now challenge your friend to make a building with a number you pick.

- Look on Google Images for some pictures of cars, trucks, planes or boats. Make a replica with the construction set. Photograph your models.

- Tape record some instructions for building a model. Invite a friend or an adult to follow your instructions. How good were they?

- Find some instruction sheets for making models. Look at how instructions are drawn. Now draw some instructions for a new model. Test them out before asking someone else to build the model. Don't forget to number the stages and pieces.

- The train in the photo on this page is life size! How many bricks do you think it needed to make it? Could you make a smaller replica?

- Challenge yourself and a few friends to make a model that uses all the pieces in the box. This may take several days!

Materials, equipment suppliers, websites, books and other references

Construction sets of unit blocks are available from all **educational suppliers**. There is a huge variety and range of types in suppliers catalogues and on their websites. Many suppliers have 'own brand' versions of generic construction sets which are often cheaper, but may have other disadvantages. As with all educational equipment, you will get what you pay for - buy the best you can afford. For instance:
ASCO: www.ascoeducational.co.uk have Babybric and Sticklebricks as well as Lego and Duplo. They also have Young Engineer and Mecanico, versions of the traditional Meccano kits.
Consortium groups can often offer class or group Lego and other sets with huge numbers of pieces. Add some more specialised pieces, wheels, people, trees etc. from local suppliers or the Lego website www.lego.com for variety and inspiration. This site also has hundreds of ideas and pictures of Lego models to explore and a free magazine. Click through to 'educators'.

For images of Lego and other construction models made by adults and children, try **Google Images**. Just enter the name of the construction set, or 'Lego model'. You could also try 'construction' 'tower' 'machine' 'bricks' 'brickwall' etc. To see more about the brick train on this page, Google 'brick train sculpture uk' then click through to the Darlington website. You could also try Google or other search engines for images of brick towers, chimneys, light bricks, glass bricks, paving blocks to see how bricks fit together and tessellate, or try Legoland.

For brick suppliers try www.brick.org.uk or www.archinet.co.uk for brickmakers near you - you could ask for samples and use these for real bricklaying.

Books for young readers interested in new ideas for construction kits:
Lego Crazy action Contraptions; Don Rathien; Klutz
Lego Builder's Guide; A Bedford; No Starch Press
and for some picture books for inspiration, search 'build your own house' on **Amazon**.

Curriculum coverage grid overleaf

Potential NC KS1 Curriculum Coverage through the provocations suggested for construction sets.

Literacy	Lit 1 speak	Lit 2 listen	Lit 3 group	Lit 4 drama	Lit 5 word	Lit 6 spell	Lit 7 text1	Lit 8 text2	Lit 9 text3	Lit10 text4	Lit11 sentence	Lit12 presentation
	1.1	2.1	3.1	4.1	5.1	6.1	7.1	8.1	9.1	10.1	11.1	12.1
	1.2	2.2	3.2	4.2	5.2	6.2	7.2	8.2	9.2	10.2	11.2	12.2

Numeracy	Num 1 U&A	Num 2 count	Num 3 number	Num 4 calculate	Num 5 shape	Num 6 measure	Num 7 data
	1.1	2.1	3.1	4.1	5.1	6.1	7.1
	1.2	2.2	3.2	4.2	5.2	6.2	7.2

This chart has been included to help you track the objectives from the **Key Stage 1 curriculum**, which the children may cover as they work on projects, challenges and provocations using **construction sets**.

A full version of the KS1 PoS objectives appears on Pages 69-74, a photocopiable version is included on Page 8.

Science

	SC1 Enquiry			SC2 Life processes					SC3 Materials		SC4 Phys processes		
	Sc1.1	Sc1.2	Sc1.3	Sc2.1	Sc2.2	Sc2.3	Sc2.4	Sc2.5	Sc3.1	Sc3.2	Sc4.1	Sc4.2	Sc4.3
	1.1a	1.2a	1.3a	2.1a	2.2a	2.3a	2.4a	2.5a	3.1a	3.2a	4.1a	4.2a	4.3a
	1.1b	1.2b	1.3b	2.1b	2.2b	2.3b	2.4b	2.5b	3.1b	3.2b	4.1b	4.2b	4.3b
	1.1c	1.2c	1.3c	2.1c	2.2c	2.3c		2.5c	3.1c		4.1c	4.2c	4.3c
	1.1d				2.2d				3.1d				4.3d
					2.2e								
					2.2f								
					2.2g								

ICT

	ICT 1 finding out		ICT 2 ideas	ICT 3 reviewing	ICT 4 breadth
	1.1a	1.2a	2a	3a	4a
	1.1b	1.2b	2b	3b	4b
	1.1c	1.2c	2c	3c	4c
		1.2d			

D&T

	D&T 1 developing	D&T 2 tool use	D&T 3 evaluating	D&T 4 materials	D&T 5 breadth
	1a	2a	3a	4a	5a
	1b	2b	3b	4b	5b
	1c	2c			5c
	1d	2d			
	1e	2e			

History

	H1 chronology	H2 events, people	H3 interpret	H4 enquire	H5 org & comm	H6 breadth
	1a	2a	3a	4a	5a	6a
	1b	2b		4b		6b
						6c
						6d

Geography

	G1.1 & G1.2 enquiry		G2 places	G3 processes	G4 environment	G5 breadth
	1.1a	1.2a	2a	3a	4a	5a
	1.1b	1.2b	2b	3b	4b	5b
	1.1c	1.2c	2c			5c
	1.1d	1.2d	2d			5d
			2e			

Music

	M1 performing	M2 composing	M3 appraising	M4 listening	M5 breadth
	1a	2a	3a	4a	5a
	1b	2b	3b	4b	5b
	1c			4c	5c
					5d

PHSE & C

	PSHEC1 conf & resp	PSHEC2 citizenship	PSHEC3 health	PSHEC4 relationships
	1a	2a	3a	4a
	1b	2b	3b	4b
	1c	2c	3c	4c
	1d	2d	3d	4d
	1e	2e	3e	4e
		2f	3f	
		2g	3g	
		2h		

Art & Design

	A&D1 ideas	A&D2 making	A&D3 evaluating	A&D4 materials	A&D5 breadth
	1a	2a	3a	4a	5a
	1b	2b	3b	4b	5b
		2c		4c	5c
					5d

PE

	PE1 devel skills	PE2 apply skills	PE3 evaluate	PE4 fitness	PE5 breadth
	1a	2a	3a	4a	5a dance
	1b	2b	3b	4b	5b games
		2c	3c		5c gym

Critical skills	Thinking Skills
problem solving	observing
decision making	classifying
critical thinking	prediction
creative thinking	making inferences
communication	problem solving
organisation	drawing conclusions
management	
leadership	

Sawn Branches

Sawn branches

Previous experience in the Foundation Stage

Collections of sawn branches provide a cheap and easy way to extend children's experience of construction with natural materials. They may already have experience of these from the Foundation Stage:

*   in free play indoors and out of doors;
*   combined with small world (to make habitats, buildings, roadways, bridges and tunnels);
*   combined with fantasy worlds (dinosaurs, princes and princesses, wizards and dragons);
*   combined with malleable materials to make habitats for toys, creatures, vehicles;
*   to count, classify, solve spatial problems
*   to explore spatial relationships in 3D;
*   to balance and build, exploring abstract and imaginative construction.

Pause for thought

In the early stages of working with these materials it is crucial to continue to observe the children. Only by doing this can you set developmentally appropriate challenges and provocations. The ideas listed here are offered as suggestions; the most exciting challenges will arise from children's own interests and motivations, which will only become apparent as you spend time with them, watching and joining them in their play. As you do this, you will be moving between the three interconnecting roles of observer, co-player, extender described below, and will be able to decide what you need to do next to take the learning forward.

The responsive adult (see page 5)

In three interconnecting roles, the responsive adult will be:

*   observing
*   listening
*   interpreting

observer

*   **modelling**
*   **playing alongside**
*   **offering suggestions**
*   **responding sensitively**
*   **initiating with care!**

co-player

*   discussing ideas
*   sharing thinking
*   modelling new skills
*   asking open questions
*   being an informed extender
*   instigating ideas & thoughts
*   supporting children as they make links in learning
*   making possibilities evident
*   introducing new ideas and resources
*   offering challenges and provocations

extender

Offering challenges and provocations - some ideas:

*   ? Can you make a castle of branches?
*   ? Can you make a wooden man or a robot?
*   ? Can you build a house for the witch from Hansel and Gretel?
*   ? Could you build a garage for this vehicle?
*   ? How do they make log cabins? Look on the Internet for some pictures.
*   ? Look at some photos of buildings made from logs and planks. Now make one yourself.
*   ? Who might live here? Offering a picture of a log cabin or tree house.
*   ? Add Gaffer tape or duct tape and build a dinosaur or forest monster.
*   ? Draw a plan for a building and take photos of each stage for a book or presentation.
*   ? Use figures to retell the story of 'The Billy Goats Gruff,' 'Little Red Riding Hood,' 'The Gruffalo'.
*   ? Add small world or fantasy figures and film or photograph your own story scenes.
*   ? Build a maze and take aerial photos. Then create a book of different sorts of mazes made with different construction materials. Which work best?
*   ? Using some sawn branches, try making towers, bridges and tunnels for small world animals or people. Can you make a town or a castle?
*   ? Find a piece of fabric and drape it over sawn branches to make landscapes for stories and adventures. Take some photos of your creations and the stories you invent.

Ready for more?

- Make a film with characters.
- Try a longer project: Design and build a structure. Measure, cut and prepare your own wood.
- Use larger branches and build a den or other structure big enough to get inside.
- Combine small or bigger branches with fabrics to make huts, tents, dens for small world people, action figures or real children.
- Use sawn branches to make letters, pictures, words. Use smaller ones to make labels, signs and notices.
- Use smaller sawn branches to make marks and write messages in mud, sand, clay or foam.
- Get some of the pencils that are made from twigs and explore how they are made.
- Use sawn branches with sand, gravel or water to make more complicated scenes and structures, with bridges, pools, slopes and caves.
- Collect sticks, branches and other fallen wood when you go on walks, and encourage children to do this too. This will expand your collection and its possibilities.

Materials, equipment suppliers, websites, books and other references

The children could help you to make your own sets of these sawn branches. Make sure the ends are smooth, and splinters are sanded off. If you use natural branches you can leave the bark on. Try to get different sizes and thicknesses, even quite big logs are are great to build with if they are cut into slices.

There is a log cabin construction set that is traditional in American homes and echoes their frontier history. **Lincoln Logs** is a kit for making model log cabins. It is available from www.constructiontoys.com Other sites for ideas of woodland and other activities involving construction with natural materials are:

Forest Schools: www.forestschools.com
Forest Education: www.foresteducation.org.uk
Yorkshire Sculpture Park: www.ysp.co.uk
Learning Through Landscapes: ww.ltl.org.uk
For images of buildings try **Google Images** 'log cabin' 'rustic furniture' 'logs' 'logpile' 'log sculpture'. Log cabins and how to build them: www.thorlogcabins.co.uk orwww.loghomebuilders.org.uk and www.twigpencils.co.uk will find just that!

The Forestry Commission website will have local addresses of places where you can go and make things with wood and wood products. Your local telephone directory will lead you to nearby sawmills or woodyards where you might be lucky in finding free or cheap materials.

Some **book** titles:
Build Your own Low Cost Log Home; Roger Hard; Garden Way
The Cabin Book; Linda Paul; Universe
and an **Amazon** search for treehouses, dens, huts will bring up other titles.

Carving is a more risky hobby, but the simple challenges of sanding, sawing, tying and sticking twigs and branches together to make gadgets and sculptures will fascinate and absorb many children.

Curriculum coverage grid overleaf

Potential NC KS1 Curriculum Coverage through the provocations suggested for sawn branches

Literacy

Literacy	Lit 1 speak	Lit 2 listen	Lit 3 group	Lit 4 drama	Lit 5 word	Lit 6 spell	Lit 7 text1	Lit 8 text2	Lit 9 text3	Lit10 text4	Lit11 sentence	Lit12 presentation
	1.1	2.1	3.1	4.1	5.1	6.1	7.1	8.1	9.1	10.1	11.1	12.1
	1.2	2.2	3.2	4.2	5.2	6.2	7.2	8.2	9.2	10.2	11.2	12.2

Numeracy

Numeracy	Num 1 U&A	Num 2 count	Num 3 number	Num 4 calculate	Num 5 shape	Num 6 measure	Num 7 data
	1.1	2.1	3.1	4.1	5.1	6.1	7.1
	1.2	2.2	3.2	4.2	5.2	6.2	7.2

This chart has been included to help you track the objectives from the **Key Stage 1 curriculum**, which the children may cover as they work on projects, challenges and provocations using **sawn branches**.

A full version of the KS1 PoS objectives appears on Pages 69-74, a photocopiable version is included on Page 8.

Science

Science	SC1 Enquiry			SC2 Life processes					SC3 Materials		SC4 Phys processes		
	Sc1.1	Sc1.2	Sc1.3	Sc2.1	Sc2.2	Sc2.3	Sc2.4	Sc2.5	Sc3.1	Sc3.2	Sc4.1	Sc4.2	Sc4.3
	1.1a	1.2a	1.3a	2.1a	2.2a	2.3a	2.4a	2.5a	3.1a	3.2a	4.1a	4.2a	4.3a
	1.1b	1.2b	1.3b	2.1b	2.2b	2.3b	2.4b	2.5b	3.1b	3.2b	4.1b	4.2b	4.3b
	1.1c	1.2c	1.3c	2.1c	2.2c	2.3c		2.5c	3.1c		4.1c	4.2c	4.3c
	1.1d				2.2d				3.1d				4.3d
					2.2e								
					2.2f								
					2.2g								

ICT

ICT	ICT 1 finding out	ICT 2 ideas	ICT 3 reviewing	ICT 4 breadth
	1.1a	1.2a	2a	3a	4a
	1.1b	1.2b	2b	3b	4b
	1.1c	1.2c	2c	3c	4c
	1.2d			

D&T

D&T	D&T 1 developing	D&T 2 tool use	D&T 3 evaluating	D&T 4 materials	D&T 5 breadth
	1a	2a	3a	4a	5a
	1b	2b	3b	4b	5b
	1c	2c			5c
	1d	2d			
	1e	2e			

History

History	H1 chronology	H2 events, people	H3 interpret	H4 enquire	H5 org & comm	H6 breadth
	1a	2a	3a	4a	5a	6a
	1b	2b		4b		6b
						6c
						6d

Geography

Geography	G1.1 & G1.2 enquiry		G2 places	G3 processes	G4 environment	G5 breadth
	1.1a	1.2a	2a	3a	4a	5a
	1.1b	1.2b	2b	3b	4b	5b
	1.1c	1.2c	2c			5c
	1.1d	1.2d	2d			5d
			2e			

Music

Music	M1 performing	M2 composing	M3 appraising	M4 listening	M5 breadth
	1a	2a	3a	4a	5a
	1b	2b	3b	4b	5b
	1c			4c	5c
					5d

PHSE & C

PHSE & C	PSHEC1 conf & resp	PSHEC2 citizenship	PSHEC3 health	PSHEC4 relationships
	1a	2a	3a	4a
	1b	2b	3b	4b
	1c	2c	3c	4c
	1d	2d	3d	4d
	1e	2e	3e	4e
		2f	3f	
		2g	3g	
		2h		

Art & Design

Art & Design	A&D1 ideas	A&D2 making	A&D3 evaluating	A&D4 materials	A&D5 breadth
	1a	2a	3a	4a	5a
	1b	2b	3b	4b	5b
		2c		4c	5c
					5d

PE

PE	PE1 devel skills	PE2 apply skills	PE3 evaluate	PE4 fitness	PE5 breadth
	1a	2a	3a	4a	5a dance
	1b	2b	3b	4b	5b games
		2c	3c		5c gym

Critical skills	Thinking Skills
problem solving	observing
decision making	classifying
critical thinking	prediction
creative thinking	making inferences
communication	problem solving
organisation	drawing conclusions
management	
leadership	

Off-cuts and sanding blocks

Off-cuts and sanding blocks

Previous experience in the Foundation Stage

Offcuts of wood are cheap and varied. Combined with sanding blocks, they provide an interesting variation for building and exploring without tools. Children may have had experience of these:

* in free play indoors and out of doors;
* combined with small world people and other figures to make habitats, roadways, bridges and tunnels;
* with sand and malleable materials to make structures;
* to explore spatial relationships in three dimensions;
* to classify, count and order;
* to explore pattern;
* to make slopes, walkways, slides and ramps for vehicles and objects, exploring sliding, rolling and balancing.

Pause for thought

In the early stages of working with these materials it is crucial to continue to observe the children. Only by doing this can you set developmentally appropriate challenges and provocations. The ideas listed here are offered as suggestions; the most exciting challenges will arise from children's own interests and motivations, which will only become apparent as you spend time with them, watching and joining them in their play. As you do this, you will be moving between the three interconnecting roles of observer, co-player, extender described below, and will be able to decide what you need to do next to take the learning forward.

The responsive adult (see page 5)

In three interconnecting roles, the responsive adult will be:

* observing
* listening
* interpreting

observer

* modelling
* playing alongside
* offering suggestions
* responding sensitively
* initiating with care!

co-player

* discussing ideas
* sharing thinking
* modelling new skills
* asking open questions
* being an informed extender
* instigating ideas & thoughts
* supporting children as they make links in learning
* making possibilities evident
* introducing new ideas and resources
* offering challenges and provocations

extender

Offering challenges and provocations - some ideas:

? Can you build a block of flats?
? What is the highest structure you can build? Measure it and make a chart to see who can build the highest.
? Can you design and build some different symmetrical buildings?
? Can you make a pattern using all the pieces?
? Add tape or other joining materials - can you make Spaghetti Junction.
? After looking at some photos of motorways, bridges and junctions, make a roadway or motorway with a series of junctions and bridges. Test it with toy cars.
? Using the sanding blocks as supports, make an apartment block with a series of rooms for Playmobil or dolls' house people.
? Build an assault course for small world figures, superheroes or Action Man.
? Construct a series of jumps for a gymkhana, a dog show etc. Add small world horses, My Little Pony, dogs.
? Make a multi-storey car park with many floors. Add ramps and bridges. Test it with vehicles.
? Use the planks to explore how things roll and slide.
? Make a museum or display of favourite objects or toys.
? Make a bookshelf for some of the books in your classroom. How can you stop the books falling over? How can you make your bookshelves taller by adding more shelves? How can you make the bookshelves safe?

Ready for more?

- Choose a heavy object. Now make a bridge that will carry that weight.

- Build replicas of ancient buildings such as the Great Wall of China, The Coliseum, the Acropolis. Find ways of making columns and other supports for the planks and blocks.

- Build a department store or a shopping mall with window displays.

- Make furniture with the pieces - chairs, tables, beds. Use fabric scraps for bedclothes, tablecloths etc. Put the furniture in a cardboard box house with windows and doors. Add small world people to make a doll's house or other habitat for people or characters.

- Use larger wood off-cuts in your outside area to make constructions or sculptures on a larger scale or to make bigger versions of the ones suggested here. You could involve an artist.

- Find out how staircases are made. You could use Google to help you. Now try making a staircase of your own, using glue if you need it.

- Can you make a toy slide for a doll, soft toy or superhero?

Materials, equipment suppliers, websites, books and other references

It is important to find and protect local sources of offcuts of timber! Ask the parents and others in the school community to help. DIY dads and mums, local small business builders, DIY and hardware shops, even asking at building sites or for wood from skips can provide you with off-cuts of all sorts of wood.

Add as many cheap sanding blocks as you can afford - these are sponge or cork blocks covered with sandpaper, available from DIY supermarkets and sometimes in packs from 'Pound' shops.

Some sets of wooden construction bricks, such as www.communityplaythings.co.uk have planks and blocks, but doing it yourself will provide much more interest and challenge for children in Key Stage 1. Children can sand the pieces to remove rough edges and the resulting set will provide endless fun in making roads, buildings and other structures.

For images of the sorts of buildings made from flat pieces with modular supports, try Google Images, starting with 'spaghetti junction' 'motorway' 'motorway bridge' 'carpark' 'coliseum' 'acropolis' 'great wall of China' 'wooden climbing frames'.

Try looking for ladder suppliers, stairs (including spiral staircases), scaffolding, wooden houses, fencing using Google or other search engines. Woodworking activities, tools, tips, ideas for children and books from www.kidscanmakeit.com

Some suitable books for younger readers include:
Build Your Own Birdhouse; K Wienberger; Scholastic
Woodworking for Kids, 40 projects; Kevin McGuire; Stirling Juvenile
www.leevalley.com has goggles and tools, plus a book called Boy Craft (try to ignore the title!) containing simple projects for young children.

Curriculum coverage grid overleaf

Potential NC KS1 Curriculum Coverage through the provocations suggested for offcuts and sanding blocks

Literacy	Lit 1 speak	Lit 2 listen	Lit 3 group	Lit 4 drama	Lit 5 word	Lit 6 spell	Lit 7 text1	Lit 8 text2	Lit 9 text3	Lit10 text4	Lit11 sentence	Lit12 presentation
	1.1	2.1	3.1	4.1	5.1	6.1	7.1	8.1	9.1	10.1	11.1	12.1
	1.2	2.2	3.2	4.2	5.2	6.2	7.2	8.2	9.2	10.2	11.2	12.2

Numeracy	Num 1 U&A	Num 2 count	Num 3 number	Num 4 calculate	Num 5 shape	Num 6 measure	Num 7 data
	1.1	2.1	3.1	4.1	5.1	6.1	7.1
	1.2	2.2	3.2	4.2	5.2	6.2	7.2

This chart has been included to help you track the objectives from the **Key Stage 1 curriculum**, which the children may cover as they work on projects, challenges and provocations using **offcuts and sanding blocks**.
A full version of the KS1 PoS objectives appears on Pages 69-74, a photocopiable version is included on Page 8.

Science	Sc1.1	Sc1.2	Sc1.3	Sc2.1	Sc2.2	Sc2.3	Sc2.4	Sc2.5	Sc3.1	Sc3.2	Sc4.1	Sc4.2	Sc4.3
	SC1 Enquiry			SC2 Life processes					SC3 Materials		SC4 Phys processes		
	1.1a	1.2a	1.3a	2.1a	2.2a	2.3a	2.4a	2.5a	3.1a	3.2a	4.1a	4.2a	4.3a
	1.1b	1.2b	1.3b	2.1b	2.2b	2.3b	2.4b	2.5b	3.1b	3.2b	4.1b	4.2b	4.3b
	1.1c	1.2c	1.3c	2.1c	2.2c	2.3c		2.5c	3.1c		4.1c	4.2c	4.3c
	1.1d				2.2d				3.1d				4.3d
					2.2e								
					2.2f								
					2.2g								

ICT	ICT 1 finding out		ICT 2 ideas	ICT 3 reviewing	ICT 4 breadth
	1.1a	1.2a	2a	3a	4a
	1.1b	1.2b	2b	3b	4b
	1.1c	1.2c	2c	3c	4c
		1.2d			

D&T	D&T 1 developing	D&T 2 tool use	D&T 3 evaluating	D&T 4 materials	D&T 5 breadth
	1a	2a	3a	4a	5a
	1b	2b	3b	4b	5b
	1c	2c			5c
	1d	2d			
	1e	2e			

History	H1 chronology	H2 events, people	H3 interpret	H4 enquire	H5 org & comm	H6 breadth
	1a	2a	3a	4a	5a	6a
	1b	2b		4b		6b
						6c
						6d

Geography	G1.1 & G1.2 enquiry		G2 places	G3 processes	G4 environment	G5 breadth
	1.1a	1.2a	2a	3a	4a	5a
	1.1b	1.2b	2b	3b	4b	5b
	1.1c	1.2c	2c			5c
	1.1d	1.2d	2d			5d
			2e			

Music	M1 performing	M2 composing	M3 appraising	M4 listening	M5 breadth
	1a	2a	3a	4a	5a
	1b	2b	3b	4b	5b
	1c			4c	5c
					5d

PHSE & C	PSHEC1 conf & resp	PSHEC2 citizenship	PSHEC3 health	PSHEC4 relationships
	1a	2a	3a	4a
	1b	2b	3b	4b
	1c	2c	3c	4c
	1d	2d	3d	4d
	1e	2e	3e	4e
		2f	3f	
		2g	3g	
		2h		

Art & Design	A&D1 ideas	A&D2 making	A&D3 evaluating	A&D4 materials	A&D5 breadth
	1a	2a	3a	4a	5a
	1b	2b	3b	4b	5b
		2c		4c	5c
					5d

PE	PE1 devel skills	PE2 apply skills	PE3 evaluate	PE4 fitness	PE5 breadth
	1a	2a	3a	4a	5a dance
	1b	2b	3b	4b	5b games
		2c	3c		5c gym

Critical skills	Thinking Skills
problem solving	observing
decision making	classifying
critical thinking	prediction
creative thinking	making inferences
communication	problem solving
organisation	drawing conclusions
management	
leadership	

Delta sand, clay, mud

Delta Sand, clay, mud

Previous experience in the Foundation Stage

Sand, clay and mud are familiar materials in the Foundation Stage; Delta Sand is a mouldable version of sand. All children should have had regular experience of these natural materials:

* in free play with and without tools, making pies, tunnels, holes and caves;
* to dig, pile, make castles and roadways;
* to make castles and use with moulds to make 3D shapes;
* to scoop, shape and pile with simple tools;
* to make environments and landscapes for small world play;
* to make simple models and sculptures which have a semi-permanent nature;
* in imaginative play, as food, gifts, objects;
* where offered, to make more permanent structures (in self hardening or Newclay).

Pause for thought

In the early stages of working with these materials it is crucial to continue to observe the children. Only by doing this can you set developmentally appropriate challenges and provocations. The ideas listed here are offered as suggestions; the most exciting challenges will arise from children's own interests and motivations, which will only become apparent as you spend time with them, watching and joining them in their play. As you do this, you will be moving between the three interconnecting roles of observer, co-player, extender described below, and will be able to decide what you need to do next to take the learning forward.

The responsive adult (see page 5)

In three interconnecting roles, the responsive adult will be:

* observing
* listening
* interpreting

* **modelling**
* **playing alongside**
* **offering suggestions**
* **responding sensitively**
* **initiating with care!**

* discussing ideas
* sharing thinking
* modelling new skills
* asking open questions
* being an informed extender
* instigating ideas & thoughts
* supporting children as they make links in learning
* making possibilities evident
* introducing new ideas and resources
* offering challenges and provocations

Offering challenges and provocations - some ideas:

? Can you make a structure with clay that is taller than a ruler?

? Which 2D or 3D shapes can you make easily with clay?

? Find a way to make bricks with clay that are all the same size. Dry your bricks in the sun or in a cool oven and then use them to make buildings.

? What happens to clay or mud when it dries? How can you find out? How can you do a fair test? Take photos of the process for a book or display.

? Can you make a house with Teifoc bricks? How can you make a roof for your house?

? Use mud to stick Teifoc bricks together. Test the strength of this method.

? Can you make a house of mud for one of the pigs in the story of the Three Little Pigs?

? Use Teifoc, Delta Sand or real bricks to explore the best way of making a wall.

? What is the best way of making the surface of clay or mud smooth?

? Find some tools or sticks and explore making marks in clay or mud.

? Make lots of balls of clay by rolling pieces in your hands. Now see how you could use these balls to make towers and pyramids.

? Roll clay into balls or cylinders and make some beads. How can you make the holes for the string?

? Roll out some clay and cut some flat squares and rectangles. Can you use these pieces to make buildings. How can you fix them together?

Ready for more?

- Look at some pictures or some real plant pots. How are they made? Could you make some?

- Get a clay plant pot and suspend it to make a bell. What do you need to make it work?

- Make some sausages or snakes from clay. Can you make these into a plate, a bowl or a sculpture?

- Use Teifoc bricks to explore making tunnels and caves. Can you make a round tunnel?

- How can you make coloured clay? Try some different ways and decide which is best.

- Make a tile from clay or mud and decorate it by using sticks or other items to scratch patterns on the surface. Which tool works best?

- Dilute some clay or mud with water - what happens? Can you get the water out again? How?

- Roll some clay flat. Can you make the flat sheet stand on its edge? Use this method to make a sculpture or mobile. You could cut shapes out of the clay piece, or make patterns on the surface. Dry your sculpture in the sun or on a radiator. What happens as it dries? Take some photos of the changes.

Materials, equipment suppliers, websites, books and other references

Suppliers of equipment and resources:
Clay should be available through usual school suppliers or a local consortium. Self hardening clay is available from www.newclay.co.uk Teifoc (picture on left) available from www.321toys.co.uk or www.teifoc.com
Delta Sand (mouldable sand) from www.deltasand.com or toy suppliers.

For images of clay, mud and sand sculpture and structures try Google Images 'mud sculpture' 'heligan' 'Antony Gormley' 'mudhut' 'clay tiles' 'plant pot' 'terracotta army' 'cob cottage' 'teifoc'.

Try a Google web search for 'antony gormley' and follow the websites to the Tate gallery/another place/Crosby Beach (his statues on a beach) or Field (a room full of tiny clay people).
Or find www.wealdown.co.uk (the Weald and Downland Museum in Sussex) for an outdoor virtual tour of all sorts of ancient buildings including some with wattle and daub walls (a mixture of mud and straw or sticks).
Cob cottages also have mud walls www.cobcottage.com will show you some examples and the way they are made. It may inspire the children to make their own model houses.

Some DVDs:
Lost Gardens of Heligan; Tim Smit
Antony Gormley; John Hutchinson; Contemporary Artists
Some suitable books include:
Homes and Houses; Usborne
Buildings of Earth and Straw; Bruce king; Ecological Design Press
The Hand Sculpted House; Ianto Evans; Realgoods, Solar Living
Ceramics for Kids; Mary Ellis; Lark Books

Curriculum coverage grid overleaf

Potential NC KS1 Curriculum Coverage through the provocations suggested for clay, mud, Delta Sand.

Literacy

	Lit 1 speak	Lit 2 listen	Lit 3 group	Lit 4 drama	Lit 5 word	Lit 6 spell	Lit 7 text1	Lit 8 text2	Lit 9 text3	Lit10 text4	Lit11 sentence	Lit12 presentation
	1.1	2.1	3.1	4.1	5.1	6.1	7.1	8.1	9.1	10.1	11.1	12.1
	1.2	2.2	3.2	4.2	5.2	6.2	7.2	8.2	9.2	10.2	11.2	12.2

Numeracy

	Num 1 U&A	Num 2 count	Num 3 number	Num 4 calculate	Num 5 shape	Num 6 measure	Num 7 data
	1.1	2.1	3.1	4.1	5.1	6.1	7.1
	1.2	2.2	3.2	4.2	5.2	6.2	7.2

This chart has been included to help you track the objectives from the **Key Stage 1 curriculum**, which the children may cover as they work on projects, challenges and provocations using **clay, mud and Delta sand**.

A full version of the KS1 PoS objectives appears on Pages 69-74, a photocopiable version is included on Page 8.

Science

	SC1 Enquiry			SC2 Life processes					SC3 Materials		SC4 Phys processes		
	Sc1.1	Sc1.2	Sc1.3	Sc2.1	Sc2.2	Sc2.3	Sc2.4	Sc2.5	Sc3.1	Sc3.2	Sc4.1	Sc4.2	Sc4.3
	1.1a	1.2a	1.3a	2.1a	2.2a	2.3a	2.4a	2.5a	3.1a	3.2a	4.1a	4.2a	4.3a
	1.1b	1.2b	1.3b	2.1b	2.2b	2.3b	2.4b	2.5b	3.1b	3.2b	4.1b	4.2b	4.3b
	1.1c	1.2c	1.3c	2.1c	2.2c	2.3c		2.5c	3.1c		4.1c	4.2c	4.3c
	1.1d				2.2d				3.1d				4.3d
					2.2e								
					2.2f								
					2.2g								

ICT

	ICT 1 finding out		ICT 2 ideas	ICT 3 reviewing	ICT 4 breadth
	1.1a	1.2a	2a	3a	4a
	1.1b	1.2b	2b	3b	4b
	1.1c	1.2c	2c	3c	4c
		1.2d			

History

	H1 chronology	H2 events, people	H3 interpret	H4 enquire	H5 org & comm	H6 breadth
	1a	2a	3a	4a	5a	6a
	1b	2b		4b		6b
						6c
						6d

Geography

	G1.1 & G1.2 enquiry		G2 places	G3 processes	G4 environment	G5 breadth
	1.1a	1.2a	2a	3a	4a	5a
	1.1b	1.2b	2b	3b	4b	5b
	1.1c	1.2c	2c			5c
	1.1d	1.2d	2d			5d
			2e			

D&T

	D&T 1 developing	D&T 2 tool use	D&T 3 evaluating	D&T 4 materials	D&T 5 breadth
	1a	2a	3a	4a	5a
	1b	2b	3b	4b	5b
	1c	2c			5c
	1d	2d			
	1e	2e			

Music

	M1 performing	M2 composing	M3 appraising	M4 listening	M5 breadth
	1a	2a	3a	4a	5a
	1b	2b	3b	4b	5b
	1c			4c	5c
					5d

PHSE & C

	PSHEC1 conf & resp	PSHEC2 citizenship	PSHEC3 health	PSHEC4 relationships
	1a	2a	3a	4a
	1b	2b	3b	4b
	1c	2c	3c	4c
	1d	2d	3d	4d
	1e	2e	3e	4e
		2f	3f	
		2g	3g	
		2h		

Art & Design

	A&D1 ideas	A&D2 making	A&D3 evaluating	A&D4 materials	A&D5 breadth
	1a	2a	3a	4a	5a
	1b	2b	3b	4b	5b
		2c		4c	5c
					5d

PE

	PE1 devel skills	PE2 apply skills	PE3 evaluate	PE4 fitness	PE5 breadth
	1a	2a	3a	4a	5a dance
	1b	2b	3b	4b	5b games
		2c	3c		5c gym

Critical skills	Thinking Skills
problem solving	observing
decision making	classifying
critical thinking	prediction
creative thinking	making inferences
communication	problem solving
organisation	drawing conclusions
management	
leadership	

Fabric, ribbons, string and threads

Fabric, ribbon, string, threads

Previous experience in the Foundation Stage

Many Foundation Stage classes use these resources as creative tool, and children are encouraged to work freely with these in a variety of ways. These may have included:

* free play indoors and out of doors;
* combined with soft toys and dolls that can be wrapped, draped, dressed;
* in role play to dress up, make settings and shelters;
* for dance and movement;
* combined with glue, and scissors to create pictures, collages and other objects;
* to weave or tie in fences, railings, netting;
* combined with beads, sequins, buttons, braid, lace, wool etc. to make patterns and decorative creations;
* to create hangings and mobiles.

Pause for thought

In the early stages of working with these materials it is crucial to continue to observe the children. Only by doing this can you set developmentally appropriate challenges and provocations. The ideas listed here are offered as suggestions; the most exciting challenges will arise from children's own interests and motivations, which will only become apparent as you spend time with them, watching and joining them in their play. As you do this, you will be moving between the three interconnecting roles of observer, co-player, extender described below, and will be able to decide what you need to do next to take the learning forward.

The responsive adult (see page 5)

In three interconnecting roles, the responsive adult will be:

* observing
* listening
* interpreting

observer

* **modelling**
* **playing alongside**
* **offering suggestions**
* **responding sensitively**
* **initiating with care!**

co-player

* discussing ideas
* sharing thinking
* modelling new skills
* asking open questions
* being an informed extender
* instigating ideas & thoughts
* supporting children as they make links in learning
* making possibilities evident
* introducing new ideas and resources
* offering challenges and provocations

extender

Offering challenges and provocations - some ideas:

NOTE: Before you present children with provocations and challenges, make sure you have modelled the skills and techniques of joining and fixing that they may need.

? Can you make a hat/coat/shoes for this soft toy/doll?
? Can you design and make:
    a bag or purse for yourself?
    a hat for a special occasion?
    a pair of shoes for a giant?
? Using a piece of hessian or a wide strip of sheeting, can you make a class wall hanging with a particular theme? (seasonal, connected with a current topic, a particular colour)
? Can you make a finger or glove puppet or a simple string puppet?
? Or can you make a picture for the classroom, the quiet area, the book corner?
? How could you make a waterproof or weatherproof picture or hanging for the wall outside?
? Use fabrics and ribbons to make a book mark for a favourite book.
? After a walk or visit, use the things you have found to make a hanging or weaving to display with your follow-up work.
? Look at some pictures of wrapping artists (try Googling 'Christo'). Then wrap some familiar objects with thin fabric, either in sheets or torn into strips.
? Find out how to make plaits. Now plait some ribbons or strings to make a hanging or a belt for yourself.

Ready for more?

👌 Suspend a garden cane or length of doweling from the ceiling or a window frame. Hang long strips of fabric from this and fix the other end of each to a second dowel to keep them steady. Work together to use this as the warp for a class or group weaving.

👌 If you have railings or a fence in your outside area, use this as a base for tying or weaving with fabric strips, ribbons, string, wool.

👌 Find an old bicycle wheel. Use this to create a wheel weaving, by threading ribbons and strings round, through and between the spokes.

👌 Buy or beg a bead or plastic strip curtain to use as a basis for a hanging or weaving.

👌 Plan and host a fashion show or an exhibition where you can showcase the things you have made.

👌 Use some long thin pieces of fabric to make tents, dens and shelters of all sizes and shapes. Fasten them together with pegs or clips.

👌 Tear some fabric into strips and use these to make an Egyptian mummy by bandaging a toy or superhero doll.

Materials, equipment suppliers, websites, books and other references

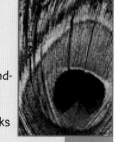

Although you can get all the resources you need from educational suppliers, it is a very expensive way to do it! It really is much better to get ribbons, strings, lace, wool, buttons, fabrics and other decorative materials from bargain sources such as:

* market stalls
* 'sale' baskets in ribbon, button and fabric shops
* florists (for ends of rolls of florist's ribbon)
* charity shops (good for buttons)
* parents and other community members (ask everyone you know to collect the spare buttons sewn inside many new clothes, and you will get a superb supply!)
* if you have a rummage sale at school, cut off the buttons from the left-over clothes
* or try the crafters section of www.ebay.co.uk where you could get some good bargains.

For a special treat try:
Texere Yarns www.texere.co.uk or www.vvrouleaux.com for all sorts of yarns, braids, beads & other trimmings. The Bead Shop www.thebeadshop.co.uk and their online store www.beadworks.co.uk.
and for ideas of what to make, try Google Images 'fabric collage', 'wall hanging', 'handmade purse', 'hat making', 'weaving'. Or search for 'weaving' for supplies and ideas.

If you get fascinated by wrapping, try www.annelyjudafineart.co.uk and look at works by Christo and Jeanne Claude, who wrap whole buildings, islands, canyons and bridges. Or put 'Andy Goldsworthy' in Google Web and look at his 'Dandelion Line'

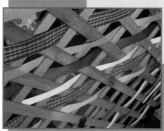

Books:
Art Forms in Nature; Ernest Haeckel; Dover Press
Natures Playground; Fiona Danks; Frances Lincoln

Curriculum coverage grid overleaf

Another idea

Soak thin fabric in wallpaper paste, squeeze or drain excess paste and drape the fabric pieces over simple (waterproof) objects. As the fabric dries, it will stiffen, and when removed, will hold the form. Experiment with uses of this new technique, you can make whole landscapes!

Potential NC KS1 Curriculum Coverage through the provocations suggested for fabric, ribbons, string etc.

Literacy

	Lit 1 speak	Lit 2 listen	Lit 3 group	Lit 4 drama	Lit 5 word	Lit 6 spell	Lit 7 text1	Lit 8 text2	Lit 9 text3	Lit10 text4	Lit11 sentence	Lit12 presentation
Literacy	1.1	2.1	3.1	4.1	5.1	6.1	7.1	8.1	9.1	10.1	11.1	12.1
	1.2	2.2	3.2	4.2	5.2	6.2	7.2	8.2	9.2	10.2	11.2	12.2

Numeracy

	Num 1 U&A	Num 2 count	Num 3 number	Num 4 calculate	Num 5 shape	Num 6 measure	Num 7 data
Numeracy	1.1	2.1	3.1	4.1	5.1	6.1	7.1
	1.2	2.2	3.2	4.2	5.2	6.2	7.2

Science

	SC1 Enquiry			SC2 Life processes					SC3 Materials		SC4 Phys processes		
	Sc1.1	Sc1.2	Sc1.3	Sc2.1	Sc2.2	Sc2.3	Sc2.4	Sc2.5	Sc3.1	Sc3.2	Sc4.1	Sc4.2	Sc4.3
Science	1.1a	1.2a	1.3a	2.1a	2.2a	2.3a	2.4a	2.5a	3.1a	3.2a	4.1a	4.2a	4.3a
	1.1b	1.2b	1.3b	2.1b	2.2b	2.3b	2.4b	2.5b	3.1b	3.2b	4.1b	4.2b	4.3b
	1.1c	1.2c	1.3c	2.1c	2.2c	2.3c		2.5c	3.1c		4.1c	4.2c	4.3c
	1.1d				2.2d				3.1d				4.3d
					2.2e								
					2.2f								
					2.2g								

ICT

	ICT 1 finding out		ICT 2 ideas	ICT 3 reviewing	ICT 4 breadth
ICT	1.1a	1.2a	2a	3a	4a
	1.1b	1.2b	2b	3b	4b
	1.1c	1.2c	2c	3c	4c
		1.2d			

D&T

	D&T 1 developing	D&T 2 tool use	D&T 3 evaluating	D&T 4 materials	D&T 5 breadth
D&T	1a	2a	3a	4a	5a
	1b	2b	3b	4b	5b
	1c	2c			5c
	1d	2d			
	1e	2e			

History

	H1 chronology	H2 events, people	H3 interpret	H4 enquire	H5 org & comm	H6 breadth
History	1a	2a	3a	4a	5a	6a
	1b	2b		4b		6b
						6c
						6d

Geography

	G1.1 & G1.2 enquiry		G2 places	G3 processes	G4 environment	G5 breadth
Geography	1.1a	1.2a	2a	3a	4a	5a
	1.1b	1.2b	2b	3b	4b	5b
	1.1c	1.2c	2c			5c
	1.1d	1.2d	2d			5d
			2e			

Music

	M1 performing	M2 composing	M3 appraising	M4 listening	M5 breadth
Music	1a	2a	3a	4a	5a
	1b	2b	3b	4b	5b
	1c			4c	5c
					5d

PHSE & C

	PSHEC1 conf & resp	PSHEC2 citizenship	PSHEC3 health	PSHEC4 relationships
PHSE & C	1a	2a	3a	4a
	1b	2b	3b	4b
	1c	2c	3c	4c
	1d	2d	3d	4d
	1e	2e	3e	4e
		2f	3f	
		2g	3g	
		2h		

Art & Design

	A&D1 ideas	A&D2 making	A&D3 evaluating	A&D4 materials	A&D5 breadth
Art & Design	1a	2a	3a	4a	5a
	1b	2b	3b	4b	5b
		2c		4c	5c
					5d

PE

	PE1 devel skills	PE2 apply skills	PE3 evaluate	PE4 fitness	PE5 breadth
PE	1a	2a	3a	4a	5a dance
	1b	2b	3b	4b	5b games
		2c	3c		5c gym

Critical skills	Thinking Skills
problem solving	observing
decision making	classifying
critical thinking	prediction
creative thinking	making inferences
communication	problem solving
organisation	drawing conclusions
management	
leadership	

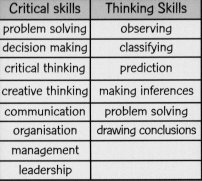

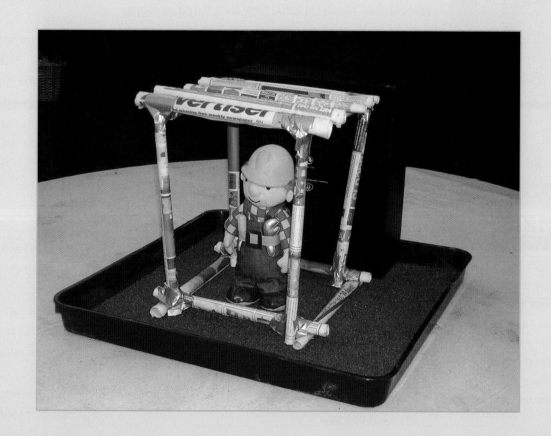

Newspaper and tape

Newspaper and tape

Previous experience in the Foundation Stage

Newspaper is another free resource used in the Foundation Stage. It may have been offered in sheet form, as strips or squares, or as papier mache. These may have included:

* supported work with adults in exploring the properties and possibilities of newspaper for building structures and supports by rolling and taping;
* free play indoors and outside;
* used flat with paste to make 3D models and sculptures;
* using scrunched or folded newspaper to stuff or support containers in construction;
* spatial problems and secure structures;
* wrapping or covering other materials such as boxes and tubes to strengthen or join them.

Pause for thought

In the early stages of working with these materials it is crucial to continue to observe the children. Only by doing this can you set developmentally appropriate challenges and provocations. The ideas listed here are offered as suggestions; the most exciting challenges will arise from children's own interests and motivations, which will only become apparent as you spend time with them, watching and joining them in their play. As you do this, you will be moving between the three interconnecting roles of observer, co-player, extender described below, and will be able to decide what you need to do next to take the learning forward.

The responsive adult (see page 5)

In three interconnecting roles, the responsive adult will be:

* observing
* listening
* interpreting

observer

* modelling
* playing alongside
* offering suggestions
* responding sensitively
* initiating with care!

co-player

* discussing ideas
* sharing thinking
* modelling new skills
* asking open questions
* being an informed extender
* instigating ideas & thoughts
* supporting children as they make links in learning
* making possibilities evident
* introducing new ideas and resources
* offering challenges and provocations

extender

Offering challenges and provocations - some ideas:

? Make the highest or longest structure you can by rolling newspapers and taping them together.
? Can you make a stand to display a model car or truck for an exhibition?
? Can you build a multi-storey car park?
? Can you make a tunnel from newspaper?
? Can you make a newspaper bridge to join two surfaces - from table to table, or between two towers of bricks?
? Use newspaper to make chairs, beds and other furniture for toys and puppets.
? Build a swing for a superhero or small soft toy.
? Build structures with curves, triangular shapes, rectangular spaces etc.
? Make a funfair ride - such as a big wheel or a swing-boat, using thinner rolls of paper and sellotape.
? Build a bridge to carry this weight (a car, train, boat).
? Make newspaper rolls and tubes into trees and plants. How tall can you make them? Can you make them taller than you? Find out how to make leaves by fringing the top of a roll of paper.
? Can you use the structures to make miniature trees and plants, railways, bridges or rides.
? Why don't we use newspaper to make buildings? Explore what happens to your newspaper constructions in wind and rain. Can you make newspaper waterproof? Take some photos of your experiments.

Ready for more?

- Build a structure with walls, perhaps using sheets of newspaper as well as rolls.

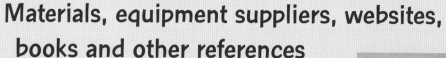

- Build a structure that incorporates rectangular, triangular <u>and</u> curved shapes.
- Build a structure big enough to get inside.
- Build a spaceship, car or train for a toy (Action Man, a superhero, a Playmobil figure).
- Investigate different sorts of newspaper and magazine paper to see which is strongest or easiest to work with, which makes the steadiest buildings.
- Test the strength of different papers to see which ones will stand up to wind and rain. Test the papers outside to find which is best.
- Explore scrunched-up newspaper, either:
  - as a construction in itself;
  - secured with tape to make structures;
  - scrunched and taped, with flat sheets pasted over the top. This makes light but solid objects, structures, landscapes or figures. When they are dry, the surface can be painted.

Materials, equipment suppliers, websites, books and other references

Newspaper and tape are two of the easiest and cheapest resources you can offer for construction. Younger children may find masking tape easier to use and tear than clear sticky tape, and you can get cheap rolls of masking tape at 'pound' shops.

Ask everyone you know to collect newspaper for you, you will be surprised how much you need for these projects and experiments. And encourage the children to recycle any spares and early efforts after they have photographed them.

Google Images responds well to 'newspaper art', newspaper butterflies', 'newspaper collage', and some inspiration may come by trying 'bridge', 'railway bridge', suspension bridge', 'gantry', 'crane', 'reinforced concrete', 'concrete pillar', 'playground swing', 'swing boat', 'big wheel'. Also try some of these in

www.wikipedia.org to get reference material and pictures.

www.art-tek.co.uk (click through to education/projects) has some good examples of bridges and tracks made from newspaper and tape.

If you make papier mache or landscapes with newspaper, try Google images for 'Tracey Island', 'Land of the Dinosaurs', 'Treasure Island' for some inspiration.

www.cleapss.org.uk (Consortium of LAs for the provision of Science Services) supports science and technology in schools. Visit their website for their primary newsletters and ideas for projects.

Curriculum coverage grid overleaf

Literacy

	Lit 1 speak	Lit 2 listen	Lit 3 group	Lit 4 drama	Lit 5 word	Lit 6 spell	Lit 7 text1	Lit 8 text2	Lit 9 text3	Lit10 text4	Lit11 sentence	Lit12 presentation
	1.1	2.1	3.1	4.1	5.1	6.1	7.1	8.1	9.1	10.1	11.1	12.1
	1.2	2.2	3.2	4.2	5.2	6.2	7.2	8.2	9.2	10.2	11.2	12.2

Numeracy

	Num 1 U&A	Num 2 count	Num 3 number	Num 4 calculate	Num 5 shape	Num 6 measure	Num 7 data
	1.1	2.1	3.1	4.1	5.1	6.1	7.1
	1.2	2.2	3.2	4.2	5.2	6.2	7.2

This chart has been included to help you track the objectives from the **Key Stage 1 curriculum**, which the children may cover as they work on projects, challenges and provocations using **newspaper and tape**.
A full version of the KS1 PoS objectives appears on Pages 69-74, a photocopiable version is included on Page 8.

Science

	SC1 Enquiry			SC2 Life processes					SC3 Materials		SC4 Phys processes		
	Sc1.1	Sc1.2	Sc1.3	Sc2.1	Sc2.2	Sc2.3	Sc2.4	Sc2.5	Sc3.1	Sc3.2	Sc4.1	Sc4.2	Sc4.3
	1.1a	1.2a	1.3a	2.1a	2.2a	2.3a	2.4a	2.5a	3.1a	3.2a	4.1a	4.2a	4.3a
	1.1b	1.2b	1.3b	2.1b	2.2b	2.3b	2.4b	2.5b	3.1b	3.2b	4.1b	4.2b	4.3b
	1.1c	1.2c	1.3c	2.1c	2.2c	2.3c		2.5c	3.1c		4.1c	4.2c	4.3c
	1.1d				2.2d				3.1d				4.3d
					2.2e								
					2.2f								
					2.2g								

ICT

	ICT 1 finding out		ICT 2 ideas	ICT 3 reviewing	ICT 4 breadth
	1.1a	1.2a	2a	3a	4a
	1.1b	1.2b	2b	3b	4b
	1.1c	1.2c	2c	3c	4c
		1.2d			

D&T

	D&T 1 developing	D&T 2 tool use	D&T 3 evaluating	D&T 4 materials	D&T 5 breadth
	1a	2a	3a	4a	5a
	1b	2b	3b	4b	5b
	1c	2c			5c
	1d	2d			
	1e	2e			

History

	H1 chronology	H2 events, people	H3 interpret	H4 enquire	H5 org & comm	H6 breadth
	1a	2a	3a	4a	5a	6a
	1b	2b		4b		6b
						6c
						6d

Geography

	G1.1 & G1.2 enquiry		G2 places	G3 processes	G4 environment	G5 breadth
	1.1a	1.2a	2a	3a	4a	5a
	1.1b	1.2b	2b	3b	4b	5b
	1.1c	1.2c	2c			5c
	1.1d	1.2d	2d			5d
			2e			

Music

	M1 performing	M2 composing	M3 appraising	M4 listening	M5 breadth
	1a	2a	3a	4a	5a
	1b	2b	3b	4b	5b
	1c			4c	5c
					5d

PHSE & C

	PSHEC1 conf & resp	PSHEC2 citizenship	PSHEC3 health	PSHEC4 relationships
	1a	2a	3a	4a
	1b	2b	3b	4b
	1c	2c	3c	4c
	1d	2d	3d	4d
	1e	2e	3e	4e
		2f	3f	
		2g	3g	
		2h		

Art & Design

	A&D1 ideas	A&D2 making	A&D3 evaluating	A&D4 materials	A&D5 breadth
	1a	2a	3a	4a	5a
	1b	2b	3b	4b	5b
		2c		4c	5c
					5d

PE

	PE1 devel skills	PE2 apply skills	PE3 evaluate	PE4 fitness	PE5 breadth
	1a	2a	3a	4a	5a dance
	1b	2b	3b	4b	5b games
		2c	3c		5c gym

Critical skills	Thinking Skills
problem solving	observing
decision making	classifying
critical thinking	prediction
creative thinking	making inferences
communication	problem solving
organisation	drawing conclusions
management	
leadership	

Paper and card
(without joining materials)

Paper and card

Previous experience in the Foundation Stage

Paper and card are staple materials in all classrooms. They are often used with glue, clips and other fixing devices. Children may also have explored paper and card without joining materials in:

* free play indoors and outside;
* to fold, bend and roll;
* to explore balance and rigidity, making the sheets stand up;
* to join by slotting, piling, balancing;
* activities involving curling, fringing, tearing and crumpling;
* making holes, piercing, punching, cutting with different sorts of scissors;
* for weaving;
* in simple wrapping and covering.

Pause for thought

In the early stages of working with these materials it is crucial to continue to observe the children. Only by doing this can you set developmentally appropriate challenges and provocations. The ideas listed here are offered as suggestions; the most exciting challenges will arise from children's own interests and motivations, which will only become apparent as you spend time with them, watching and joining them in their play. As you do this, you will be moving between the three interconnecting roles of observer, co-player, extender described below, and will be able to decide what you need to do next to take the learning forward.

The responsive adult (see page 5)

In three interconnecting roles, the responsive adult will be:

observer

* observing
* listening
* interpreting

co-player

* **modelling**
* **playing alongside**
* **offering suggestions**
* **responding sensitively**
* **initiating with care!**

extender

* discussing ideas
* sharing thinking
* modelling new skills
* asking open questions
* being an informed extender
* instigating ideas & thoughts
* supporting children as they make links in learning
* making possibilities evident
* introducing new ideas and resources
* offering challenges and provocations

Offering challenges and provocations - some ideas:

? Can you make a piece of paper stand on its edge?
? Do you know how to make a fan? How many different sorts of fans can you make with paper and card?
? Build some structures with a pack of cards (no glue or fixings!). Take photos of the different structures you make.
? Use paper or card to make a box or container (no glue or fixings).
? Find a book on origami or search for origami on the Internet. Make some origami paper folding shapes and animals.
? How can you make paper curl?
? Explore fringing by tearing or using scissors.
? Explore making slots and holes in card and paper. Does this make it easier to make structures and objects? Cut come rectangles of card or stiff paper and make slots in the edges to fit them together. How high can you build?
? How many different ways can you join two pieces of paper or card without using clips, pins or glue?
? Find out how to make a zigzag book. Explore making different sizes and shapes of zigzag books. Which size and shape works best? Take photos of your experiments.
? Make some tubes from paper. How can you fix them without using glue? Can you use the tubes and some flat sheets to make a building? How strong is you building? How could you make it stronger?

Ready for more?

- Can you make a mask from paper? How can you make it fit your face? Explore ways of making the holes for eyes and nose in the right places so you can see out?

- What is the best sort of paper for curling? For fringing? For folding? Record your experiments in photos or a chart.

- Use what you find out about curling and folding to make a sculpture. Look up 'paper sculpture' on Google Images for ideas of things to make. Display your sculptures and try writing instructions so other people can learn how to do it.

- Cut circles of paper into spirals. Find a way of hanging these up. Watch them move.

- Can you make a paper aeroplane? Find out how to make some more by asking your friends, your family, or using books or the Internet.

- Explore making paper flowers. Try using crepe paper and tissue or wrapping paper. Find a way to display your work.

- Cut some circles from paper or thin card. How can you make the circles into cones? Make cones of different sizes and heights.

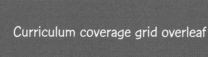

Materials, equipment suppliers, websites, books and other references

The preparation for these activities is important. Children need access to as many different sorts, sizes and colours of paper and card that you can find. Much of this range can be cheap or free, so don't forget to include:

- the sides from cardboard cartons and boxes
- the backs of pads
- packaging from clothes and food
- used envelopes and junk mail (this is often printed on tough paper)
- crepe, tissue, greaseproof, foil, wrapping paper, streamers, cellophane, sugar paper
- origami paper
- old playing cards
- birthday and Christmas cards
- wallpaper and lining paper in rolls.

Contact local printers and the parents for spare or recycled paper and card, and use your local Scrapstore (find a directory on ww.childrensscrapstore.co.uk), or try www.uniquescrapstore.com the first on-line scrapstore.

CABE (the Commission for Architecture and the Built Environment) at www.cabe.org.uk celebrate architecture and have images of the cardboard school building pictured below. They also support projects in schools.

Try Google Images 'torn paper', 'paper aeroplanes', 'paper lanterns', 'paper sculpture', card sculpture', 'house of cards', 'weaving', 'paper lantern', 'origami', or Google Web 'paper decoration', 'origami'.

www.paperfolding.com will give you some ideas and diagrams for models.

Books:

Origami for Beginners; Dover Press

www.tarquinbooks.com have technology ideas and books on paper structures

Curriculum coverage grid overleaf

This school building is made of cardboard!

Potential NC KS1 Curriculum Coverage through the provocations suggested for paper and card

Literacy	Lit 1 speak	Lit 2 listen	Lit 3 group	Lit 4 drama	Lit 5 word	Lit 6 spell	Lit 7 text1	Lit 8 text2	Lit 9 text3	Lit10 text4	Lit11 sentence	Lit12 presentation
	1.1	2.1	3.1	4.1	5.1	6.1	7.1	8.1	9.1	10.1	11.1	12.1
	1.2	2.2	3.2	4.2	5.2	6.2	7.2	8.2	9.2	10.2	11.2	12.2

Numeracy	Num 1 U&A	Num 2 count	Num 3 number	Num 4 calculate	Num 5 shape	Num 6 measure	Num 7 data
	1.1	2.1	3.1	4.1	5.1	6.1	7.1
	1.2	2.2	3.2	4.2	5.2	6.2	7.2

This chart has been included to help you track the objectives from the **Key Stage 1 curriculum**, which the children may cover as they work on projects, challenges and provocations using **paper and card**.
A full version of the KS1 PoS objectives appears on Pages 69-74, a photocopiable version is included on Page 8.

Science	SC1 Enquiry			SC2 Life processes					SC3 Materials		SC4 Phys processes		
	Sc1.1	Sc1.2	Sc1.3	Sc2.1	Sc2.2	Sc2.3	Sc2.4	Sc2.5	Sc3.1	Sc3.2	Sc4.1	Sc4.2	Sc4.3
	1.1a	1.2a	1.3a	2.1a	2.2a	2.3a	2.4a	2.5a	3.1a	3.2a	4.1a	4.2a	4.3a
	1.1b	1.2b	1.3b	2.1b	2.2b	2.3b	2.4b	2.5b	3.1b	3.2b	4.1b	4.2b	4.3b
	1.1c	1.2c	1.3c	2.1c	2.2c	2.3c		2.5c	3.1c		4.1c	4.2c	4.3c
	1.1d				2.2d				3.1d				4.3d
					2.2e								
					2.2f								
					2.2g								

ICT	ICT 1 finding out		ICT 2 ideas	ICT 3 reviewing	ICT 4 breadth
	1.1a	1.2a	2a	3a	4a
	1.1b	1.2b	2b	3b	4b
	1.1c	1.2c	2c	3c	4c
		1.2d			

D&T	D&T 1 developing	D&T 2 tool use	D&T 3 evaluating	D&T 4 materials	D&T 5 breadth
	1a	2a	3a	4a	5a
	1b	2b	3b	4b	5b
	1c	2c			5c
	1d	2d			
	1e	2e			

History	H1 chronology	H2 events, people	H3 interpret	H4 enquire	H5 org & comm	H6 breadth
	1a	2a	3a	4a	5a	6a
	1b	2b		4b		6b
						6c
						6d

Geography	G1.1 & G1.2 enquiry		G2 places	G3 processes	G4 environment	G5 breadth
	1.1a	1.2a	2a	3a	4a	5a
	1.1b	1.2b	2b	3b	4b	5b
	1.1c	1.2c	2c			5c
	1.1d	1.2d	2d			5d
			2e			

Music	M1 performing	M2 composing	M3 appraising	M4 listening	M5 breadth
	1a	2a	3a	4a	5a
	1b	2b	3b	4b	5b
	1c			4c	5c
					5d

PHSE & C	PSHEC1 conf & resp	PSHEC2 citizenship	PSHEC3 health	PSHEC4 relationships
	1a	2a	3a	4a
	1b	2b	3b	4b
	1c	2c	3c	4c
	1d	2d	3d	4d
	1e	2e	3e	4e
		2f	3f	
		2g	3g	
		2h		

Art & Design	A&D1 ideas	A&D2 making	A&D3 evaluating	A&D4 materials	A&D5 breadth
	1a	2a	3a	4a	5a
	1b	2b	3b	4b	5b
		2c		4c	5c
					5d

PE	PE1 devel skills	PE2 apply skills	PE3 evaluate	PE4 fitness	PE5 breadth
	1a	2a	3a	4a	5a dance
	1b	2b	3b	4b	5b games
		2c	3c		5c gym

Critical skills	Thinking Skills
problem solving	observing
decision making	classifying
critical thinking	prediction
creative thinking	making inferences
communication	problem solving
organisation	drawing conclusions
management	
leadership	

Cane, willow, hazel whips

Cane, willow, hazel whips

Previous experience in the Foundation Stage

Cane is the thin, flexible stems of bamboo or reeds often used for furniture and baskets.
Willow or hazel whips are flexible branches traditionally used for basket making and fencing. They are also planted, as they root easily. Some children may have explored these materials in the Foundation Stage through:

* free play indoors or out of doors;
* exploring or constructing in 3 dimensions;
* creating natural structures by tying, weaving and growing living willow or hazel;
* combining cane and whips with fabrics and natural materials by weaving and tying;
* making nests, containers, simple baskets.

Pause for thought

In the early stages of working with these materials it is crucial to continue to observe the children. Only by doing this can you set developmentally appropriate challenges and provocations. The ideas listed here are offered as suggestions; the most exciting challenges will arise from children's own interests and motivations, which will only become apparent as you spend time with them, watching and joining them in their play. As you do this, you will be moving between the three interconnecting roles of observer, co-player, extender described below, and will be able to decide what you need to do next to take the learning forward.

The responsive adult (see page 5)

In three interconnecting roles, the responsive adult will be:

observer

* observing
* listening
* interpreting

co-player

* **modelling**
* **playing alongside**
* **offering suggestions**
* **responding sensitively**
* **initiating with care!**

extender

* discussing ideas
* sharing thinking
* modelling new skills
* asking open questions
* being an informed extender
* instigating ideas & thoughts
* supporting children as they make links in learning
* making possibilities evident
* introducing new ideas and resources
* offering challenges and provocations

Offering challenges and provocations - some ideas:

If children have not had previous experience of using these materials, you may need to model ways of bending, manipulating and joining the canes safely and creatively. You can incorporate fabric, ribbon and natural materials with twigs, canes and whips so children can explore them. Once children have had this experience, they will be able to explore the possibilities themselves.

? Design and make a series of two dimensional hangings to decorate the windows or for an outside area. Add some coloured cellophane, acetate or other papers to your structure.

? Can you build homes or dens for small world or fantasy characters?

? Can you design and make a 3 dimensional hanging or sculpture, by tying the canes together? You could add ribbons, strings, feathers or other natural objects.

? Design and make some containers for a variety of purposes - to carry fruit, eggs, bread etc. Take photos of your containers.

? Working in pairs or small groups, make a small structure each, then join them together to make a bigger one.

? Make a waterproof structure by adding fabric or plastic (bubble wrap is fun!).

? Look at your outdoor area and decide where a willow, cane or twig structure could enhance the environment. Make structures together for these places.

? Find some very bendy twigs or sticks and see if you can plait or twist them into a structure.

? Look at different sorts of nests (of birds and animals). Try making some nests from sticks and other natural materials.

Ready for more?

- Collect a range of 'dream catchers', mobiles and other hanging structures, and use these to inspire children's ideas for their own creations.

- Use whips and canes to make larger structures out of doors. Combine these with light fabrics and other materials, and use them for places of quiet reflection.

- Use the canes to make structures for climbing plants - runner beans, Morning Glory, Mile a Minute vine, tomatoes, or cucumbers.

- Send for some living willow whips and design and make a living willow structure in your school grounds.

- Ask a local artist or sculptor to come and work with the children on an outdoor project, using natural materials.

- Bring materials back from walks and visits to incorporate in your work.

- Make simple wigwams and cover these with thin fabric. How can you make the wigwams waterproof and windproof. Experiment with paints, diluted glues, plastic. Decide which is best.

- Design a structure and work with two friends to help you build it.

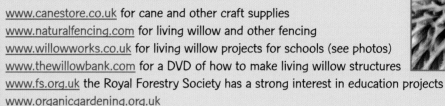

Materials, equipment suppliers, websites, books and other references

Cane for baskets and other related crafts from:

www.canestore.co.uk for cane and other craft supplies
www.naturalfencing.com for living willow and other fencing
www.willowworks.co.uk for living willow projects for schools (see photos)
www.thewillowbank.com for a DVD of how to make living willow structures
www.fs.org.uk the Royal Forestry Society has a strong interest in education projects
www.organicgardening.org.uk
www.bbc.co.uk/gardening/gardening_with_children for ideas and projects
www.hazelwattle.com and click on photos for fencing and wattle making
www.englishwillowbaskets.co.uk for basket making supplies and lots of photos of baskets
www.bushcraftexpeditions.com click through to UK courses/junior courses for photos
www.forestschools.com Forest Schools
www.foresteducation.org.uk Forest Education

Try Google Images: 'hanging decoration', 'Andy Goldsworthy' (a sculptor who works with natural materials), 'hangings', 'willow', 'living willow', 'cane', 'wattle', 'basket', 'nest', 'den'

Some books:
Nature's Playground; Fiona Danks; Frances Lincoln
Gardening with Children; Kim Wilde; Collins
Whittling Twigs and Branches; C Lubkeman; Guild of Master Craftsmen
Leaf Man, and Red Leaf, Yellow Leaf; Lois Ehlert; Harcourt
Living Willow Structures; John Warnes; Search Press
Nature's Art Box; Kids projects; Laura Martin; Storey
Baskets; Meryl Doney; Franklin Watts
Basket Making (Start a Craft); Polly Pollock; Apple Press

Curriculum coverage grid overleaf

Literacy

Literacy	Lit 1 speak	Lit 2 listen	Lit 3 group	Lit 4 drama	Lit 5 word	Lit 6 spell	Lit 7 text1	Lit 8 text2	Lit 9 text3	Lit10 text4	Lit11 sentence	Lit12 presentation
	1.1	2.1	3.1	4.1	5.1	6.1	7.1	8.1	9.1	10.1	11.1	12.1
	1.2	2.2	3.2	4.2	5.2	6.2	7.2	8.2	9.2	10.2	11.2	12.2

Numeracy

Numeracy	Num 1 U&A	Num 2 count	Num 3 number	Num 4 calculate	Num 5 shape	Num 6 measure	Num 7 data
	1.1	2.1	3.1	4.1	5.1	6.1	7.1
	1.2	2.2	3.2	4.2	5.2	6.2	7.2

This chart has been included to help you track the objectives from the **Key Stage 1 curriculum**, which the children may cover as they work on projects, challenges and provocations using **cane, willow and hazel whips**. *A full version of the KS1 PoS objectives appears on Pages 69-74, a photocopiable version is included on Page 8.*

Science

Science	Sc1.1	Sc1.2	Sc1.3	Sc2.1	Sc2.2	Sc2.3	Sc2.4	Sc2.5	Sc3.1	Sc3.2	Sc4.1	Sc4.2	Sc4.3
(SC1 Enquiry / SC2 Life processes / SC3 Materials / SC4 Phys processes)	1.1a	1.2a	1.3a	2.1a	2.2a	2.3a	2.4a	2.5a	3.1a	3.2a	4.1a	4.2a	4.3a
	1.1b	1.2b	1.3b	2.1b	2.2b	2.3b	2.4b	2.5b	3.1b	3.2b	4.1b	4.2b	4.3b
	1.1c	1.2c	1.3c	2.1c	2.2c	2.3c		2.5c	3.1c		4.1c	4.2c	4.3c
	1.1d				2.2d				3.1d				4.3d
					2.2e								
					2.2f								
					2.2g								

ICT

ICT	ICT 1 finding out		ICT 2 ideas	ICT 3 reviewing	ICT 4 breadth
	1.1a	1.2a	2a	3a	4a
	1.1b	1.2b	2b	3b	4b
	1.1c	1.2c	2c	3c	4c
		1.2d			

D&T

D&T	D&T 1 developing	D&T 2 tool use	D&T 3 evaluating	D&T 4 materials	D&T 5 breadth
	1a	2a	3a	4a	5a
	1b	2b	3b	4b	5b
	1c	2c			5c
	1d	2d			
	1e	2e			

History

History	H1 chronology	H2 events, people	H3 interpret	H4 enquire	H5 org & comm	H6 breadth
	1a	2a	3a	4a	5a	6a
	1b	2b		4b		6b
						6c
						6d

Geography

Geography	G1.1 & G1.2 enquiry		G2 places	G3 processes	G4 environment	G5 breadth
	1.1a	1.2a	2a	3a	4a	5a
	1.1b	1.2b	2b	3b	4b	5b
	1.1c	1.2c	2c			5c
	1.1d	1.2d	2d			5d
			2e			

Music

Music	M1 performing	M2 composing	M3 appraising	M4 listening	M5 breadth
	1a	2a	3a	4a	5a
	1b	2b	3b	4b	5b
	1c			4c	5c
					5d

PHSE & C

PHSE & C	PSHEC1 conf & resp	PSHEC2 citizenship	PSHEC3 health	PSHEC4 relationships
	1a	2a	3a	4a
	1b	2b	3b	4b
	1c	2c	3c	4c
	1d	2d	3d	4d
	1e	2e	3e	4e
		2f	3f	
		2g	3g	
		2h		

Art & Design

Art & Design	A&D1 ideas	A&D2 making	A&D3 evaluating	A&D4 materials	A&D5 breadth
	1a	2a	3a	4a	5a
	1b	2b	3b	4b	5b
		2c		4c	5c
					5d

PE

PE	PE1 devel skills	PE2 apply skills	PE3 evaluate	PE4 fitness	PE5 breadth
	1a	2a	3a	4a	5a dance
	1b	2b	3b	4b	5b games
		2c	3c		5c gym

Critical skills / Thinking Skills

Critical skills	Thinking Skills
problem solving	observing
decision making	classifying
critical thinking	prediction
creative thinking	making inferences
communication	problem solving
organisation	drawing conclusions
management	
leadership	

Living willow chair before growth!

and after growth!

Living willow dome

Pebbles, Cobbles, Stones

Pebbles, cobbles, stones

Previous experience in the Foundation Stage

Pebbles and stones are traditional playthings for all children, and experience of these from gravel to cobbles is a valuable way to learn the properties of these natural materials safely and with control. In the Foundation Stage, many settings offer stones:

* in free play for sorting, building, scooping and piling;
* for sorting, grading and exploring shape, pattern, colour, texture and form;
* to carry, shift, transport in wheeled toys and other containers;
* to explore flat and three dimensional shapes and the way they fit together;
* to make simple structures, bridges, roads and gardens;
* in mosaics and tiles, setting them in sand, mud or clay.

Pause for thought

In the early stages of working with these materials it is crucial to continue to observe the children. Only by doing this can you set developmentally appropriate challenges and provocations. The ideas listed here are offered as suggestions; the most exciting challenges will arise from children's own interests and motivations, which will only become apparent as you spend time with them, watching and joining them in their play. As you do this, you will be moving between the three interconnecting roles of observer, co-player, extender described below, and will be able to decide what you need to do next to take the learning forward.

The responsive adult (see page 5)

In three interconnecting roles, the responsive adult will be:

* observing
* listening
* interpreting

observer

* modelling
* playing alongside
* offering suggestions
* responding sensitively
* initiating with care!

co-player

* discussing ideas
* sharing thinking
* modelling new skills
* asking open questions
* being an informed extender
* instigating ideas & thoughts
* supporting children as they make links in learning
* making possibilities evident
* introducing new ideas and resources
* offering challenges and provocations

extender

Offering challenges and provocations - some ideas:

? Make patterns and pictures with polished pebbles in trays of sand or mud. Look for some pictures of mosaics in books and on the Internet.

? Can you use stones to make a building without glue or mortar?

? Find some stones in your school garden, or bring some from home. Wash them, then use your collection to make a picture, structure or pattern.

? Can you make your stones into a stone museum by sorting, labelling and classifying them?

? Explore some gravel. How does it move? What is it? Look at it through a magnifying glass. Make piles, paths, mounds. Sort it for colour or size.

? Find some Blutack or plasticene. Use this to make structures with stones and pebbles.

? Look for some flat stones and use these to make bridges. Prop them up with other stones. Look for some pictures of stone bridges.

? Build some walls with stones and pebbles. Which shapes are easiest to build with?

? Look for stones and pebbles with holes in them. Thread these on a string.

? Look in your local environment for cobbled and other paved areas. Record different sorts of cobbles and stone surfaces by taking photos. Use these as ideas for your own creations.

? Collect some small round stones and use these to make paths and surfaces in miniature gardens or other models.

Ready for more?

- Use some history books to find out more about mosaics. Draw designs on squared paper, then make the mosaic with stones, or thick card cut into squares.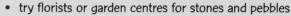

- Dig outside or at home to find some stones. Wash them and use them to make a pattern or construction. Stick them to each other or a piece of wood using strong glue.

- Find a way to test the hardness of different sorts of stones. Organise your collection to show what you found out.

- Get some aquarium gravel and find out how it behaves. Can you build or sculpt it? Look at it through a magnifying glass. What can you see? Compare this gravel with pea gravel and sand.

- Find out about stone bridges, dolmens, cairns, henges (eg Stonehenge) from the Internet or books. Try making your own.

- Take a few handfuls of stones and use these to make as many different patterns and shapes as you can. Record your work in drawings or photos. Then challenge a friend to make the same patterns.

Materials, equipment suppliers, websites, books and other references

Suppliers and sources:

Although it is illegal to take quantities of stones from rivers and beaches, you might ask every child to bring just one from their holidays for your collection. Some other ideas are:

- bags of polished stones and pebbles, and glass beads are available in many bargain shops at bargain prices
- try florists or garden centres for stones and pebbles
- DIY and garden centres usually have lots of different sorts of gravels and stones from pea gravel to cobbles and big stones for rockeries
- coloured gravel from aquarium shops makes a change, and they often have rocks of unusual shapes for imaginative constructions.

www.buystone.co.uk/pebbles have lovely pictures on the website and polished stones cheap! they also have really interesting things like fossilised wood

www.dandys.org have coloured glass and slate

www.outlandstone.co.uk sell stones and pebbles in lovely colours, look at the pictures, but you have to buy at least 25kg of each or share a bag!

www.emporiumuk.biz have a massive range of glass beads, marbles and other decorative beads.

Use **Google Images** for pictures - some suggestions for words to search: 'stone wall', 'dolmen', 'cairn', 'river bed', 'stone bridge', 'volcano', 'cobbles', 'Stonehenge', 'stone sculpture'.

Some books:
Lets Have a Look at Pebbles; Angela Royston; Heinemann
The Complete Mosaic Pebble Book; Maggie Howarth; Frances Lincoln
Stone; Andy Goldsworthy; Harry Abrahams
Wall; Andy Goldsworthy; Harry Abrahams

Curriculum coverage grid overleaf

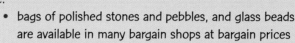
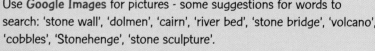

Potential NC KS1 Curriculum Coverage through the provocations suggested for pebbles and stones

Literacy	Lit 1 speak	Lit 2 listen	Lit 3 group	Lit 4 drama	Lit 5 word	Lit 6 spell	Lit 7 text1	Lit 8 text2	Lit 9 text3	Lit10 text4	Lit11 sentence	Lit12 presentation
	1.1	2.1	3.1	4.1	5.1	6.1	7.1	8.1	9.1	10.1	11.1	12.1
	1.2	2.2	3.2	4.2	5.2	6.2	7.2	8.2	9.2	10.2	11.2	12.2

Numeracy	Num 1 U&A	Num 2 count	Num 3 number	Num 4 calculate	Num 5 shape	Num 6 measure	Num 7 data
	1.1	2.1	3.1	4.1	5.1	6.1	7.1
	1.2	2.2	3.2	4.2	5.2	6.2	7.2

This chart has been included to help you track the objectives from the **Key Stage 1 curriculum**, which the children may cover as they work on projects, challenges and provocations using **pebbles and stones**.

A full version of the KS1 PoS objectives appears on Pages 69-74, a photocopiable version is included on Page 8.

Science	SC1 Enquiry			SC2 Life processes					SC3 Materials		SC4 Phys processes		
	Sc1.1	Sc1.2	Sc1.3	Sc2.1	Sc2.2	Sc2.3	Sc2.4	Sc2.5	Sc3.1	Sc3.2	Sc4.1	Sc4.2	Sc4.3
	1.1a	1.2a	1.3a	2.1a	2.2a	2.3a	2.4a	2.5a	3.1a	3.2a	4.1a	4.2a	4.3a
	1.1b	1.2b	1.3b	2.1b	2.2b	2.3b	2.4b	2.5b	3.1b	3.2b	4.1b	4.2b	4.3b
	1.1c	1.2c	1.3c	2.1c	2.2c	2.3c		2.5c	3.1c		4.1c	4.2c	4.3c
	1.1d				2.2d				3.1d				4.3d
					2.2e								
					2.2f								
					2.2g								

ICT	ICT 1 finding out		ICT 2 ideas	ICT 3 reviewing	ICT 4 breadth
	1.1a	1.2a	2a	3a	4a
	1.1b	1.2b	2b	3b	4b
	1.1c	1.2c	2c	3c	4c
		1.2d			

D&T	D&T 1 developing	D&T 2 tool use	D&T 3 evaluating	D&T 4 materials	D&T 5 breadth
	1a	2a	3a	4a	5a
	1b	2b	3b	4b	5b
	1c	2c			5c
	1d	2d			
	1e	2e			

History	H1 chronology	H2 events, people	H3 interpret	H4 enquire	H5 org & comm	H6 breadth
	1a	2a	3a	4a	5a	6a
	1b	2b		4b		6b
						6c
						6d

Geography	G1.1 & G1.2 enquiry		G2 places	G3 processes	G4 environment	G5 breadth
	1.1a	1.2a	2a	3a	4a	5a
	1.1b	1.2b	2b	3b	4b	5b
	1.1c	1.2c	2c			5c
	1.1d	1.2d	2d			5d
			2e			

Music	M1 performing	M2 composing	M3 appraising	M4 listening	M5 breadth
	1a	2a	3a	4a	5a
	1b	2b	3b	4b	5b
	1c			4c	5c
					5d

PHSE & C	PSHEC1 conf & resp	PSHEC2 citizenship	PSHEC3 health	PSHEC4 relationships
	1a	2a	3a	4a
	1b	2b	3b	4b
	1c	2c	3c	4c
	1d	2d	3d	4d
	1e	2e	3e	4e
		2f	3f	
		2g	3g	
		2h		

Art& Design	A&D1 ideas	A&D2 making	A&D3 evaluating	A&D4 materials	A&D5 breadth
	1a	2a	3a	4a	5a
	1b	2b	3b	4b	5b
		2c		4c	5c
					5d

PE	PE1 devel skills	PE2 apply skills	PE3 evaluate	PE4 fitness	PE5 breadth
	1a	2a	3a	4a	5a dance
	1b	2b	3b	4b	5b games
		2c	3c		5c gym

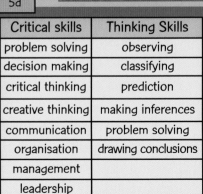

Critical skills	Thinking Skills
problem solving	observing
decision making	classifying
critical thinking	prediction
creative thinking	making inferences
communication	problem solving
organisation	drawing conclusions
management	
leadership	

Skewers, cocktail sticks
Blutack/Plasticene

Skewers, sticks and Blutack/Plasticene

Previous experience in the Foundation Stage
Thin wooden skewers such as barbecue skewers, can provide a simple activity which explores space, shape and stability. Children may have had experience of these materials:

* in free play indoors and out of doors;
* combined with small world people and animals, vehicles etc;
* combined with malleable materials such as clay or dough;
* for spatial problem solving and exploring structures;
* to experiment with joining, fixing and tying;
* combined with light fabrics and papers (net, tissue, newspaper, plastic, gauze, cellophane, greaseproof, foil etc).

Pause for thought
In the early stages of working with these materials it is crucial to continue to observe the children. Only by doing this can you set developmentally appropriate challenges and provocations. The ideas listed here are offered as suggestions; the most exciting challenges will arise from children's own interests and motivations, which will only become apparent as you spend time with them, watching and joining them in their play. As you do this, you will be moving between the three interconnecting roles of observer, co-player, extender described below, and will be able to decide what you need to do next to take the learning forward.

The responsive adult (see page 5)

In three interconnecting roles, the responsive adult will be:

* observing
* listening
* interpreting

 observer

* **modelling**
* **playing alongside**
* **offering suggestions**
* **responding sensitively**
* **initiating with care!**

co-player

* discussing ideas
* sharing thinking
* modelling new skills
* asking open questions
* being an informed extender
* instigating ideas & thoughts
* supporting children as they make links in learning
* making possibilities evident
* introducing new ideas and resources
* offering challenges and provocations

extender

Offering challenges and provocations - some ideas:

? Choose a toy vehicle, and build a structure for it - a shelter, garage or other building. Use tissue or other paper to make walls. Can you make it waterproof?

? Build a tepee or wigwam for fantasy toys.

? Can you build a structure that is:
   - long and narrow
   - as tall as you can make it
   - with curving sides?

? Build a two or three storey structure.

? Look for some pictures of buildings or structures. Use Google to look for ideas. Now make some replicas with your own materials.

? Can you use the sticks to build a robot, an alien or a fantasy figure? Add fabrics and other objects to make your figure realistic.

? Can you design and build a bird or a plane? You could use paper for feathers for a bird.

? Explore how you could make cages for animals with skewers and Blutack.

? Can you build a structure that will carry a weight? How strong can you make your structure

? Try adding string or cotton and natural objects to make a mobile from skewers.

? Build the house of sticks for the 3 Little Pigs.

? Plan and draw a labelled diagram of a building, then build it according to your plan. Take photos of each stage and make a photo book or PowerPoint presentation to show to your class

Ready for more?

👆 Soak some dried peas overnight till they are soft, and use them with cocktail sticks to make smaller versions of models and structures.

👆 Can you make some structures that move? Look on Theme Park websites to find pictures of rides. Try:
- a 'Big Wheel' from the funfair, or the London Eye;
- a seesaw;
- a swing or swing boat;
- a roundabout, swing boat or Chair-o-plane.

👆 Work in a group to make an American Indian village of tepees. Find some small world people to live there and make them clothes from thin fabric. Make a video film or photo story of your village. Research your project in books and on the Internet.

👆 Try making a larger structure with these small sticks. You could make a windmill, a rocket, a theatre for small world figures.

👆 Look at the domes on this page, and find some more by using Google. Use sticks and Blutack or soaked peas to make your own domes. What could you use for the glass?

Materials, equipment suppliers, websites, books and other references

Resources from:
Artstraws: www.artastik.co.uk or www.technologysupplies.co.uk
www.artcraft.co.uk have a huge range of craft supplies, including sticks; the site also has an index of craft sites across the UK
www.solardome.co.uk has a range of photos of geodesic domes, a section on domes for schools, and links to finding funding for projects and resources; they also provided the images for this page
www.sparkofinspiration.co.uk for construction kits with sticks and balls and magnetic sets

Google images: 'tent', 'geodesic dome', 'dome', 'bubbles', 'frame', 'disney epcot', 'greenhouse structure', 'engineering'
and **Google search** for 'eden project', 'epcot', 'frame tents', 'wigwam', 'tepee', 'marquee' for all sorts of frames for tents and other structures

www.bdp.co.uk/structures/engineering this site of a structural engineer will lead you to lots of projects - look at Crown lane School, London for a domed roof, or Devonshire Exemplar school for a rooftop playground.
This website link; www.teachernet.gov.uk/management/resourcesfinanceandbuildings/school-buildings/exemplars/primary will take you to the government school buildings examples - try Sarah Wigglesworth architects to look at plans and photos of a new primary school.

Books and Publications
Geodesic Domes; Borin van Loon; from www.tarquinbooks.com a site that has lots of books on technology, ideas for teachers, and downloadable activity sheets, as well as Geomag books.

Curriculum coverage grid overleaf

Potential NC KS1 Curriculum Coverage through the provocations suggested for skewers, sticks, Blutack

Literacy

	Lit 1 speak	Lit 2 listen	Lit 3 group	Lit 4 drama	Lit 5 word	Lit 6 spell	Lit 7 text1	Lit 8 text2	Lit 9 text3	Lit10 text4	Lit11 sentence	Lit12 presentation
Literacy	1.1	2.1	3.1	4.1	5.1	6.1	7.1	8.1	9.1	10.1	11.1	12.1
	1.2	2.2	3.2	4.2	5.2	6.2	7.2	8.2	9.2	10.2	11.2	12.2

Numeracy

	Num 1 U&A	Num 2 count	Num 3 number	Num 4 calculate	Num 5 shape	Num 6 measure	Num 7 data
Numeracy	1.1	2.1	3.1	4.1	5.1	6.1	7.1
	1.2	2.2	3.2	4.2	5.2	6.2	7.2

This chart has been included to help you track the objectives from the **Key Stage 1 curriculum**, which the children may cover as they work on projects, challenges and provocations using **skewers, sticks and Blutack**.
A full version of the KS1 PoS objectives appears on Pages 69-74, a photocopiable version is included on Page 8.

Science

	SC1 Enquiry			SC2 Life processes					SC3 Materials		SC4 Phys processes		
	Sc1.1	Sc1.2	Sc1.3	Sc2.1	Sc2.2	Sc2.3	Sc2.4	Sc2.5	Sc3.1	Sc3.2	Sc4.1	Sc4.2	Sc4.3
Science	1.1a	1.2a	1.3a	2.1a	2.2a	2.3a	2.4a	2.5a	3.1a	3.2a	4.1a	4.2a	4.3a
	1.1b	1.2b	1.3b	2.1b	2.2b	2.3b	2.4b	2.5b	3.1b	3.2b	4.1b	4.2b	4.3b
	1.1c	1.2c	1.3c	2.1c	2.2c	2.3c		2.5c	3.1c		4.1c	4.2c	4.3c
	1.1d				2.2d				3.1d				4.3d
					2.2e								
					2.2f								
					2.2g								

ICT

	ICT 1 finding out		ICT 2 ideas	ICT 3 reviewing	ICT 4 breadth
ICT	1.1a	1.2a	2a	3a	4a
	1.1b	1.2b	2b	3b	4b
	1.1c	1.2c	2c	3c	4c
		1.2d			

History

	H1 chronology	H2 events, people	H3 interpret	H4 enquire	H5 org & comm	H6 breadth
History	1a	2a	3a	4a	5a	6a
	1b	2b		4b		6b
						6c
						6d

Geography

	G1.1 & G1.2 enquiry		G2 places	G3 processes	G4 environment	G5 breadth
Geography	1.1a	1.2a	2a	3a	4a	5a
	1.1b	1.2b	2b	3b	4b	5b
	1.1c	1.2c	2c			5c
	1.1d	1.2d	2d			5d
			2e			

D&T

	D&T 1 developing	D&T 2 tool use	D&T 3 evaluating	D&T 4 materials	D&T 5 breadth
D&T	1a	2a	3a	4a	5a
	1b	2b	3b	4b	5b
	1c	2c			5c
	1d	2d			
	1e	2e			

Music

	M1 performing	M2 composing	M3 appraising	M4 listening	M5 breadth
Music	1a	2a	3a	4a	5a
	1b	2b	3b	4b	5b
	1c			4c	5c
					5d

PHSE & C

	PSHEC1 conf & resp	PSHEC2 citizenship	PSHEC3 health	PSHEC4 relationships
PHSE & C	1a	2a	3a	4a
	1b	2b	3b	4b
	1c	2c	3c	4c
	1d	2d	3d	4d
	1e	2e	3e	4e
		2f	3f	
		2g	3g	
		2h		

Art & Design

	A&D1 ideas	A&D2 making	A&D3 evaluating	A&D4 materials	A&D5 breadth
Art & Design	1a	2a	3a	4a	5a
	1b	2b	3b	4b	5b
		2c		4c	5c
					5d

PE

	PE1 devel skills	PE2 apply skills	PE3 evaluate	PE4 fitness	PE5 breadth
PE	1a	2a	3a	4a	5a dance
	1b	2b	3b	4b	5b games
		2c	3c		5c gym

Critical skills	Thinking Skills
problem solving	observing
decision making	classifying
critical thinking	prediction
creative thinking	making inferences
communication	problem solving
organisation	drawing conclusions
management	
leadership	

Cocktail sticks and soaked dried peas

Sticks, twigs, garden canes and tape

Sticks, twigs, canes & tape

Previous experience in the Foundation Stage

These materials support construction on a bigger scale. They are easily joined with string, duct tape, elastic bands or plant ties. Children may have already experienced these materials in:

* adult directed activities, particularly when gardening;
* to make dens, tents and shelters, child sized or smaller;
* to make structures for supporting plants;
* activities combining sticks and canes with fabrics to make small world settings;
* in Forest School activities to explore natural materials in natural environments.

Pause for thought

In the early stages of working with these materials it is crucial to continue to observe the children. Only by doing this can you set developmentally appropriate challenges and provocations. The ideas listed here are offered as suggestions; the most exciting challenges will arise from children's own interests and motivations, which will only become apparent as you spend time with them, watching and joining them in their play. As you do this, you will be moving between the three interconnecting roles of observer, co-player, extender described below, and will be able to decide what you need to do next to take the learning forward.

The responsive adult (see page 5)

In three interconnecting roles, the responsive adult will be:

observer

* observing
* listening
* interpreting

co-player

* modelling
* playing alongside
* offering suggestions
* responding sensitively
* initiating with care!

extender

* discussing ideas
* sharing thinking
* modelling new skills
* asking open questions
* being an informed extender
* instigating ideas & thoughts
* supporting children as they make links in learning
* making possibilities evident
* introducing new ideas and resources
* offering challenges and provocations

Offering challenges and provocations - some ideas:

? Can you use sticks or canes and tape to make a structure big enough to sit inside? How can you make it stand up by itself?

? Use canes or sticks and fabric to make a bigger den or wigwam.

? Can you make a structure with three canes? Now can you suspend something from the canes so it hangs inside the structure?

? Use two canes and a length of thin fabric to make a hanging. Decorate your hanging with natural objects and materials such as feathers, stones, leaves, twigs and flowers.

? Draw or paint a picture. Use four short canes or sticks to make a frame for your picture. Can you find a way to fix them together?

? Get some garden ties and garden sticks. Use the ties to help you make some different shapes with the sticks. Take photos of the structures you make.

? Take some photos so you can make a photo book of how to build a wigwam.

? Hang a cane up from both ends. Use it to make a decoration for your classroom by hanging things from the cane. Can you make a natural decoration? a seasonal decoration? a decoration made just from paper?

? Fix four sticks or twigs together to make a square or rectangle. Now find some string, ribbons, wool or fabric strips to make a decoration. How can you fix them to the frame?

Ready for more?

- Make a square hollow structure with 12 sticks or canes. Find the best way to fix them together. Cover the structure with fabric and hang objects inside your cave. Can you hang something in the middle of the cave? What is the best way to do this? How can you find out where the middle is? Use torches to make your cave an exciting place to be.

- Use green garden sticks to make a decorative structure outside. Explore ways of fixing it so it doesn't blow away!

- Look on pages 53/56 and make bigger versions of the ideas there.

- Make a wigwam with garden sticks or canes. How many do you need to make it stand up? Now see if you can find out which sort of seeds you could plant to grow up the wigwam of canes. Look for climbing plants or vegetables that grow fast. Make a photo or video record of your project.

- Find some thinner, flexible canes or sticks, and experiment with making tunnels by bending them. How can you fix them safely? Can you cover them with fabric or paper?

Materials, equipment suppliers, websites, books and other references

Some ideas for **resources and equipment**:

For sticks and fixing:

    Garden centres are a good source of sticks (get bamboo canes and plant supports of different lengths, green garden sticks)

    Collect fallen sticks on walks to the woods

    Ask parents and colleagues to collect sticks of all sorts and sizes

    Buy plant ties and twisties, masking tape and duct tape from bargain and 'Pound' shops

    Get some cord, rope, strong elastic bands and string to give alternatives for fixing

    Consider offering some soft wire to make hooks and hangers

www.ysp.co.uk/education/projects the site for the Yorkshire Sculpture Park where children can work with natural and found materials

www.forestschools.com the site for Forest School links and information on local projects

www.foresteducation.org www.woodcraft.org.uk www.scouts.org.uk and www.forest-arts.co.uk are other interesting sites

Google images: 'bamboo', 'wigwam', 'tepee/tipi', 'forest den', 'sticks', 'forest shelter', 'structures', 'forest schools'

Books and Publications:

365 Activities for Fitness, Food and Fun for the whole Family; Julia Sweet; McGraw Hill

Winter, Spring, Summer and Autumn Nature Activities for Children; (4 books); Irmgard Kutsch; Floris Books

Nature's Playground; Fiona Danks; Frances Lincoln

Kids Gone Camping; Cherie Winner; Creative Publishing

Kids Camp!; Laurie M Carlson; Chicago Review Press

The Little Book of Growing Things and The Little Book of Outdoor Play; Sally Featherstone; Featherstone Education

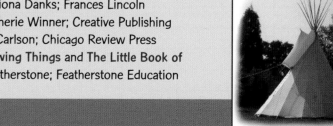
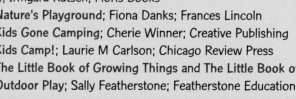

Curriculum coverage grid overleaf

Potential NC KS1 Curriculum Coverage through the provocations suggested for sticks, twigs etc

Literacy

	Lit 1 speak	Lit 2 listen	Lit 3 group	Lit 4 drama	Lit 5 word	Lit 6 spell	Lit 7 text1	Lit 8 text2	Lit 9 text3	Lit10 text4	Lit11 sentence	Lit12 presentation
Literacy	1.1	2.1	3.1	4.1	5.1	6.1	7.1	8.1	9.1	10.1	11.1	12.1
	1.2	2.2	3.2	4.2	5.2	6.2	7.2	8.2	9.2	10.2	11.2	12.2

Numeracy

	Num 1 U&A	Num 2 count	Num 3 number	Num 4 calculate	Num 5 shape	Num 6 measure	Num 7 data
Numeracy	1.1	2.1	3.1	4.1	5.1	6.1	7.1
	1.2	2.2	3.2	4.2	5.2	6.2	7.2

This chart has been included to help you track the objectives from the **Key Stage 1 curriculum**, which the children may cover as they work on projects, challenges and provocations using **sticks, twigs and canes**.
A full version of the KS1 PoS objectives appears on Pages 69-74, a photocopiable version is included on Page 8.

Science

	SC1 Enquiry			SC2 Life processes					SC3 Materials		SC4 Phys processes		
	Sc1.1	Sc1.2	Sc1.3	Sc2.1	Sc2.2	Sc2.3	Sc2.4	Sc2.5	Sc3.1	Sc3.2	Sc4.1	Sc4.2	Sc4.3
Science	1.1a	1.2a	1.3a	2.1a	2.2a	2.3a	2.4a	2.5a	3.1a	3.2a	4.1a	4.2a	4.3a
	1.1b	1.2b	1.3b	2.1b	2.2b	2.3b	2.4b	2.5b	3.1b	3.2b	4.1b	4.2b	4.3b
	1.1c	1.2c	1.3c	2.1c	2.2c	2.3c		2.5c	3.1c		4.1c	4.2c	4.3c
	1.1d				2.2d				3.1d				4.3d
					2.2e								
					2.2f								
					2.2g								

ICT

	ICT 1 finding out		ICT 2 ideas	ICT 3 reviewing	ICT 4 breadth
ICT	1.1a	1.2a	2a	3a	4a
	1.1b	1.2b	2b	3b	4b
	1.1c	1.2c	2c	3c	4c
		1.2d			

History

	H1 chronology	H2 events, people	H3 interpret	H4 enquire	H5 org & comm	H6 breadth
History	1a	2a	3a	4a	5a	6a
	1b	2b		4b		6b
						6c
						6d

Geography

	G1.1 & G1.2 enquiry		G2 places	G3 processes	G4 environment	G5 breadth
Geography	1.1a	1.2a	2a	3a	4a	5a
	1.1b	1.2b	2b	3b	4b	5b
	1.1c	1.2c	2c			5c
	1.1d	1.2d	2d			5d
			2e			

D&T

	D&T 1 developing	D&T 2 tool use	D&T 3 evaluating	D&T 4 materials	D&T 5 breadth
D&T	1a	2a	3a	4a	5a
	1b	2b	3b	4b	5b
	1c	2c			5c
	1d	2d			
	1e	2e			

Music

	M1 performing	M2 composing	M3 appraising	M4 listening	M5 breadth
Music	1a	2a	3a	4a	5a
	1b	2b	3b	4b	5b
	1c			4c	5c
					5d

PHSE & C

	PSHEC1 conf & resp	PSHEC2 citizenship	PSHEC3 health	PSHEC4 relationships
PHSE & C	1a	2a	3a	4a
	1b	2b	3b	4b
	1c	2c	3c	4c
	1d	2d	3d	4d
	1e	2e	3e	4e
		2f	3f	
		2g	3g	
		2h		

Art & Design

	A&D1 ideas	A&D2 making	A&D3 evaluating	A&D4 materials	A&D5 breadth
Art & Design	1a	2a	3a	4a	5a
	1b	2b	3b	4b	5b
		2c		4c	5c
					5d

PE

	PE1 devel skills	PE2 apply skills	PE3 evaluate	PE4 fitness	PE5 breadth
PE	1a	2a	3a	4a	5a dance
	1b	2b	3b	4b	5b games
		2c	3c		5c gym

Critical skills	Thinking Skills
problem solving	observing
decision making	classifying
critical thinking	prediction
creative thinking	making inferences
communication	problem solving
organisation	drawing conclusions
management	
leadership	

Recycled materials

Recycled materials

Previous experience in the Foundation Stage

Recycled materials, freely available to all schools are an endless source for construction and creativity on small or large scale projects. All children should have had experience with these materials in:

* making homes, houses and environments for small world figures and characters;
* constructing vehicles, buildings, containers;
* replicating the objects they see in real life;
* making props for role play or outdoor play;
* with big boxes and cartons, playing in, on and around the spaces they provide;
* using boxes for fantasy and role play;
* stacking, balancing, building with shapes;
* exploring shape, size, stability, balance and other properties in three dimensions;
* filling and emptying with objects or toys.

Pause for thought

In the early stages of working with these materials it is crucial to continue to observe the children. Only by doing this can you set developmentally appropriate challenges and provocations. The ideas listed here are offered as suggestions; the most exciting challenges will arise from children's own interests and motivations, which will only become apparent as you spend time with them, watching and joining them in their play. As you do this, you will be moving between the three interconnecting roles of observer, co-player, extender described below, and will be able to decide what you need to do next to take the learning forward.

The responsive adult (see page 5)

In three interconnecting roles, the responsive adult will be:

* observing
* listening
* interpreting

observer

* **modelling**
* **playing alongside**
* **offering suggestions**
* **responding sensitively**
* **initiating with care!**

co-player

* discussing ideas
* sharing thinking
* modelling new skills
* asking open questions
* being an informed extender
* instigating ideas & thoughts
* supporting children as they make links in learning
* making possibilities evident
* introducing new ideas and resources
* offering challenges and provocations

extender

Offering challenges and provocations - some ideas:

? Look carefully at a collection of boxes and other recycled materials. Draw a design of something to make, then make it.

? Use a big box to make a den, spaceship, house or boat.

? Can you use recycled materials to make a vehicle for a superhero? a fantasy home for a fantasy character? a farm or zoo for model animals?

? Experiment with making structures with recycled materials without using glue or tape. Who can build the tallest structure? Take photos of the best ones.

? Can you make some tunnels or waterways with recycled tubes and tape? Test your structures with toy cars, water, or marbles.

? Collect some recycled plastic objects. Use these to make an outdoor sculpture or a building, using waterproof tape to fix the parts. Put your construction outside and test whether it is weatherproof.

? Use some recycled plastic cups or yogurt pots to explore how supermarkets make different stacks and piles of packets and tins. Which is the best way to build? Take photos of the best ideas.

? Collect some plastic water bottles and explore what you can do with them. You could cut them to remove the tops and bottoms. What can you make now?

? Find some old newspapers and make some paper mache by tearing the paper into strips or squares and soaking them in paste. What can you make now?

Ready for more?

- Explore different tapes and glues with different objects and materials, which works best?

- How many different structures can you build with 100 plastic cups, without fixing them together? Explore and record all the ways you can do this, then try building again with tape or glue.

- Contact your local Scrap Store and find out what they can offer. Using a Scrap Store will make your constructions much more interesting.

- Can you make a paint that will stick to plastic cups or shiny boxes? Record your experiments and make some instructions in pictures, words or photos, so other people can do it too.

- Find some boxes and carefully take them apart, so you can find out how they are made. Use these shapes (called nets) as templates or patterns for making your own boxes.

- Use Google to find some recycled art. Use some of the ideas to help you make some creations of your own.

- Look at the chicken on this page. It is made from plastic carrier bags. How do you think it was done. Can you make one?

Materials, equipment suppliers, websites, books and other references

Some ideas for resources and equipment:

Recycled materials are free!

Ask parents, carers, local businesses - anyone you can think of to collect recycled materials for you.

Put a notice up inviting offers of CLEAN recycled materials such as:

- plastic bottles and tops, containers, cups, tubs and pots
- cardboard tubes, boxes and cones, egg boxes
- plastic and polystyrene trays, bubble wrap
- offcuts of paper and wallpaper, newspapers, junk mail and magazines
- plastic and paper carriers, paper bags
- plant pots and seed trays
- string, wool, cord and rope; sticks, twigs, small logs

Leave a box by the notice, so parents and children can drop their offerings in. Then you can sort and check them for suitability, Health and Safety and cleanliness.

Recycled Giraffe (detail) - Shiam Wilcox

www.scrapstore.co.uk and www.scrapstore.org will give you help in locating scrapstores near your setting. www.recycling-guide.org.uk/activities has recycling guidance for schools and some ideas of simple things to make

Google images: 'recycled art', 'art recycling', 'junk art', 'art from packaging', 'polystyrene sculpture', 'rubbish', 'car sculpture'

Google search: 'scrapstore', 'recycling

Or contact your local recycling centre or Council office for recycling advice, leaflets and information.

Books and Publications

Astonishing Art with Recycled Rubbish; bsmall publishing

Recycled, Re-seen; Charlene Cerny; Harry Abrahams

Recycled Crafts for Kids; Marion Elliot; Lorenz Books

Curriculum coverage grid overleaf

Potential NC KS1 Curriculum Coverage through the provocations suggested for recycled materials

Literacy

	Lit 1 speak	Lit 2 listen	Lit 3 group	Lit 4 drama	Lit 5 word	Lit 6 spell	Lit 7 text1	Lit 8 text2	Lit 9 text3	Lit10 text4	Lit11 sentence	Lit12 presentation
Literacy	1.1	2.1	3.1	4.1	5.1	6.1	7.1	8.1	9.1	10.1	11.1	12.1
	1.2	2.2	3.2	4.2	5.2	6.2	7.2	8.2	9.2	10.2	11.2	12.2

Numeracy

	Num 1 U&A	Num 2 count	Num 3 number	Num 4 calculate	Num 5 shape	Num 6 measure	Num 7 data
Numeracy	1.1	2.1	3.1	4.1	5.1	6.1	7.1
	1.2	2.2	3.2	4.2	5.2	6.2	7.2

This chart has been included to help you track the objectives from the **Key Stage 1 curriculum**, which the children may cover as they work on projects, challenges and provocations using **recycled materials**.

A full version of the KS1 PoS objectives appears on Pages 69-74, a photocopiable version is included on Page 8.

Science

	SC1 Enquiry			SC2 Life processes					SC3 Materials		SC4 Phys processes		
	Sc1.1	Sc1.2	Sc1.3	Sc2.1	Sc2.2	Sc2.3	Sc2.4	Sc2.5	Sc3.1	Sc3.2	Sc4.1	Sc4.2	Sc4.3
Science	1.1a	1.2a	1.3a	2.1a	2.2a	2.3a	2.4a	2.5a	3.1a	3.2a	4.1a	4.2a	4.3a
	1.1b	1.2b	1.3b	2.1b	2.2b	2.3b	2.4b	2.5b	3.1b	3.2b	4.1b	4.2b	4.3b
	1.1c	1.2c	1.3c	2.1c	2.2c	2.3c		2.5c	3.1c		4.1c	4.2c	4.3c
	1.1d				2.2d				3.1d				4.3d
					2.2e								
					2.2f								
					2.2g								

ICT

	ICT 1 finding out		ICT 2 ideas	ICT 3 reviewing	ICT 4 breadth
ICT	1.1a	1.2a	2a	3a	4a
	1.1b	1.2b	2b	3b	4b
	1.1c	1.2c	2c	3c	4c
		1.2d			

D&T

	D&T 1 developing	D&T 2 tool use	D&T 3 evaluating	D&T 4 materials	D&T 5 breadth
D&T	1a	2a	3a	4a	5a
	1b	2b	3b	4b	5b
	1c	2c			5c
	1d	2d			
	1e	2e			

History

	H1 chronology	H2 events, people	H3 interpret	H4 enquire	H5 org & comm	H6 breadth
History	1a	2a	3a	4a	5a	6a
	1b	2b		4b		6b
						6c
						6d

Geography

	G1.1 & G1.2 enquiry		G2 places	G3 processes	G4 environment	G5 breadth
Geography	1.1a	1.2a	2a	3a	4a	5a
	1.1b	1.2b	2b	3b	4b	5b
	1.1c	1.2c	2c			5c
	1.1d	1.2d	2d			5d
			2e			

Music

	M1 performing	M2 composing	M3 appraising	M4 listening	M5 breadth
Music	1a	2a	3a	4a	5a
	1b	2b	3b	4b	5b
	1c			4c	5c
					5d

North Tyneside Recycling Project

East Leeds Early Years Centre

PHSE & C

	PSHEC1 conf & resp	PSHEC2 citizenship	PSHEC3 health	PSHEC4 relationships
PHSE & C	1a	2a	3a	4a
	1b	2b	3b	4b
	1c	2c	3c	4c
	1d	2d	3d	4d
	1e	2e	3e	4e
		2f	3f	
		2g	3g	
		2h		

Art & Design

	A&D1 ideas	A&D2 making	A&D3 evaluating	A&D4 materials	A&D5 breadth
Art & Design	1a	2a	3a	4a	5a
	1b	2b	3b	4b	5b
		2c		4c	5c
					5d

PE

	PE1 devel skills	PE2 apply skills	PE3 evaluate	PE4 fitness	PE5 breadth
PE	1a	2a	3a	4a	5a dance
	1b	2b	3b	4b	5b games
		2c	3c		5c gym

Recycled Hippo - Shiam Wilcox

Critical skills	Thinking Skills
problem solving	observing
decision making	classifying
critical thinking	prediction
creative thinking	making inferences
communication	problem solving
organisation	drawing conclusions
management	
leadership	

Combining materials

Combining materials

Previous experience in the Foundation Stage

If children have come from a setting with a well resourced workshop area, they will have had plenty of experience of combining materials:

* in free play, indoors and outside;
* for making, homes, houses, garages and environments for toys, animals, vehicles;
* to help represent objects and experiences in their own lives;
* for balancing, stacking and building;
* in role play scenarios, for making props;
* to solve spatial problems and explore structures;
* to prop, extend and support structures built in recycled and found materials;
* to test and explore the properties of different materials.

Pause for thought

In the early stages of working with these materials it is crucial to continue to observe the children. Only by doing this can you set developmentally appropriate challenges and provocations. The ideas listed here are offered as suggestions; the most exciting challenges will arise from children's own interests and motivations, which will only become apparent as you spend time with them, watching and joining them in their play. As you do this, you will be moving between the three interconnecting roles of observer, co-player, extender described below, and will be able to decide what you need to do next to take the learning forward.

The responsive adult (see page 5)

In three interconnecting roles, the responsive adult will be:

observer

* observing
* listening
* interpreting

co-player

* **modelling**
* **playing alongside**
* **offering suggestions**
* **responding sensitively**
* **initiating with care!**

extender

* discussing ideas
* sharing thinking
* modelling new skills
* asking open questions
* being an informed extender
* instigating ideas & thoughts
* supporting children as they make links in learning
* making possibilities evident
* introducing new ideas and resources
* offering challenges and provocations

Offering challenges and provocations - some ideas:

? Can you use a combination of materials to make a robot, a fire engine, a spaceship, a dinosaur, a dalek, a tractor, a digger?

? Can you make a structure using three different sorts of materials? Decide on the materials before you start.

? Look at all the resources you have, and sort them into man made and natural materials. Can you make a structure using a combination of man made and natural materials?

? Combine materials to make a 'set' for a play about the three Billy Goats Gruff or another favourite story.

? Make a plan for a building or vehicle. List all the components you will need, and collect them together before you build your model according to your plan.

? Build a construction. Now can you cover the whole thing with something to make it look as though it has all been made from one material?

? Make a plan for a construction made from a combination of materials. Now get a friend to make the construction using your instructions.

? Get a friend to help you build the tallest or widest or longest structure you can.

? What is the highest structure you can build without using glue or tape? Now try again with tape and glue to help you make the model even higher.

? Use as many of the materials as you can to make a fantasy landscape for animals and people.

Ready for more?

- Use a combination of materials to make an item of clothing or footwear. Have a fashion show.

- Can you build a structure that lights up? You could try a cave, a lighthouse, a spaceship or a robot.

- Choose a favourite story and build a series of sets for a play or puppet show. Photograph each scene and use the computer to make a book or PowerPoint presentation.

- Can you work as a class or group to build a village, castle, space station, hospital using a whole range of bought and recycled materials? Take your time over days or a week, and make sure you have somewhere to keep your unfinished work.

- Google 'built from junk' to see how one man has built a house using other people's junk.

- Can you design and make some new and interesting constructions using several different types of paper, a range of different fabrics, just paper plates and cups, or just boxes?

- Can you design and make a storage area for all the recycled materials in your classroom to keep them tidy?

Materials, equipment suppliers, websites, books and other references

Increase your supply of recycled materials by:

* contacting local industry, shops or manufacturers;
* asking parents and members of the community to keep their eyes and ears open for sources of paper, card, boxes, ribbon etc;
* asking for used cups from water fountains, keeping paper and plastic plates;
* making sure you keep and re-use packaging of all sorts, and ask colleagues to do so too;
* asking kitchens and caretaking services if they have suitable containers (make sure they have only been used for safe materials and clean them again before use)

For images try Google Images 'buildings with junk' 'mixed media' 'mixed media sculpture' 'mixed media structures' 'junk sculpture' 'card sculpture'.

Google Web (UK sites) for 'sculpture from junk' then try these sites

www.colinmcgookin.com for a site that shows work with children

www.recyclingconsortium.org.uk a site for teachers with recycling ideas

www.198gallery.co.uk has some great planes made from junk

www.sculturebythesea.com is a site in Australia with pictures of beach sculptures.

Some suitable books for younger readers include:

Look What You Can Make with Tubes/Newspapers and Magazines/Craft Sticks/ Plastic Bottle and Tubs/Paper Plates/Boxes; Various authors; Boyds Mills Press

Building; Philip Wilkinson; DK Eyewitness

The Iron Man and The Iron Woman; Ted Hughes; Puffin Books

The Iron Giant; (DVD)

Some other books about mixed media sculpture for inspiration:

Recycled, Re-seen; Charlene Cerny; Harry Abrahams

Cast off, re-cast; Timothy Corrigan Correll; Washington University Press

Curriculum coverage grid overleaf

Potential NC KS1 Curriculum Coverage through the provocations suggested for combining materials

Literacy

	Lit 1 speak	Lit 2 listen	Lit 3 group	Lit 4 drama	Lit 5 word	Lit 6 spell	Lit 7 text1	Lit 8 text2	Lit 9 text3	Lit10 text4	Lit11 sentence	Lit12 presentation
Literacy	1.1	2.1	3.1	4.1	5.1	6.1	7.1	8.1	9.1	10.1	11.1	12.1
	1.2	2.2	3.2	4.2	5.2	6.2	7.2	8.2	9.2	10.2	11.2	12.2

Numeracy

	Num 1 U&A	Num 2 count	Num 3 number	Num 4 calculate	Num 5 shape	Num 6 measure	Num 7 data
Numeracy	1.1	2.1	3.1	4.1	5.1	6.1	7.1
	1.2	2.2	3.2	4.2	5.2	6.2	7.2

This chart has been included to help you track the objectives from the **Key Stage 1 curriculum**, which the children may cover as they work on projects, challenges and provocations using **combining materials**.

A full version of the KS1 PoS objectives appears on Pages 69-74, a photocopiable version is included on Page 8.

Science

	SC1 Enquiry			SC2 Life processes					SC3 Materials		SC4 Phys processes		
	Sc1.1	Sc1.2	Sc1.3	Sc2.1	Sc2.2	Sc2.3	Sc2.4	Sc2.5	Sc3.1	Sc3.2	Sc4.1	Sc4.2	Sc4.3
Science	1.1a	1.2a	1.3a	2.1a	2.2a	2.3a	2.4a	2.5a	3.1a	3.2a	4.1a	4.2a	4.3a
	1.1b	1.2b	1.3b	2.1b	2.2b	2.3b	2.4b	2.5b	3.1b	3.2b	4.1b	4.2b	4.3b
	1.1c	1.2c	1.3c	2.1c	2.2c	2.3c		2.5c	3.1c		4.1c	4.2c	4.3c
	1.1d				2.2d				3.1d				4.3d
					2.2e								
					2.2f								
					2.2g								

ICT

	ICT 1 finding out		ICT 2 ideas	ICT 3 reviewing	ICT 4 breadth
ICT	1.1a	1.2a	2a	3a	4a
	1.1b	1.2b	2b	3b	4b
	1.1c	1.2c	2c	3c	4c
		1.2d			

D&T

	D&T 1 developing	D&T 2 tool use	D&T 3 evaluating	D&T 4 materials	D&T 5 breadth
D&T	1a	2a	3a	4a	5a
	1b	2b	3b	4b	5b
	1c	2c			5c
	1d	2d			
	1e	2e			

History

	H1 chronology	H2 events, people	H3 interpret	H4 enquire	H5 org & comm	H6 breadth
History	1a	2a	3a	4a	5a	6a
	1b	2b		4b		6b
						6c
						6d

Geography

	G1.1 & G1.2 enquiry		G2 places	G3 processes	G4 environment	G5 breadth
Geography	1.1a	1.2a	2a	3a	4a	5a
	1.1b	1.2b	2b	3b	4b	5b
	1.1c	1.2c	2c			5c
	1.1d	1.2d	2d			5d
			2e			

Music

	M1 performing	M2 composing	M3 appraising	M4 listening	M5 breadth
Music	1a	2a	3a	4a	5a
	1b	2b	3b	4b	5b
	1c			4c	5c
					5d

North Tyneside Recycling Project

PHSE & C

	PSHEC1 conf & resp	PSHEC2 citizenship	PSHEC3 health	PSHEC4 relationships
PHSE & C	1a	2a	3a	4a
	1b	2b	3b	4b
	1c	2c	3c	4c
	1d	2d	3d	4d
	1e	2e	3e	4e
		2f	3f	
		2g	3g	
		2h		

Art & Design

	A&D1 ideas	A&D2 making	A&D3 evaluating	A&D4 materials	A&D5 breadth
Art & Design	1a	2a	3a	4a	5a
	1b	2b	3b	4b	5b
		2c		4c	5c
					5d

PE

	PE1 devel skills	PE2 apply skills	PE3 evaluate	PE4 fitness	PE5 breadth
PE	1a	2a	3a	4a	5a dance
	1b	2b	3b	4b	5b games
		2c	3c		5c gym

North Tyneside Recycling Project

Critical skills	Thinking Skills
problem solving	observing
decision making	classifying
critical thinking	prediction
creative thinking	making inferences
communication	problem solving
organisation	drawing conclusions
management	
leadership	

Curriculum Links and Resources

The following pages contain the detail for the curriculum key which appears at the end of each section of the book. The appendix consists of the following:

1. Short-hand versions of the QCA/DfES Programme of Study for Key Stage 1 in:

   > Science
   >
   > Information & Communication Technology
   >
   > Design and Technology
   >
   > History
   >
   > Geography
   >
   > Music
   >
   > Art and Design
   >
   > Physical Education

2. The suggested programme of study for Personal, Social and Health Education and Citizenship (PSHE & C)

3. The elements of the guidance for learning and teaching of Literacy and Numeracy in Years 1 and 2 (from the Primary Framework for literacy and mathematics; DfES/SureStart; Sept 2006; Ref: 02011-2006BOK-EN)

Literacy 1 speaking	Literacy 2 listening & responding	Literacy 3 group discussion & interaction	Literacy 4 drama	Literacy 5 word recognition, coding & decoding	Literacy 6 word structure & spelling	Literacy 7 understanding & interpreting texts	Literacy 8 engaging & responding to text	Literacy 9 creating and shaping texts	Literacy 10 text structure & organisation	Literacy 11 sentence structure & punctuation	Literacy 12 presentation
Year 1 **Tell stories and describe incidents from their own experience in an audible voice** **Retell stories,** ordering events using story language Interpret a text by reading aloud with some variety in pace and emphasis **Experiment with & build new stores of words** to communicate in different contexts	**Year 1** Listen with **sustained concentration,** building new stores of words in different contexts **Listen to and follow instructions** accurately, asking for help and clarification if necessary Listen to tapes or video and **express views about how a story or information has been presented**	**Year 1** **Take turns to speak, listen to** others' suggestions and talk about what they are going to do Ask and answer questions, make relevant contributions, offer suggestions and take turns **Explain their views to others** in a small group, decide how to report the group's views to the class	**Year 1** Explore familiar themes and characters through improvisation and role-play **Act out their own and well-known stories,** using voices for characters Discuss why they like a performance	**Year 1** **Recognise & use alternative ways of pronouncing the graphemes already taught,** for example, that the grapheme 'g' is pronounced differently in 'get' and 'gem'; the grapheme 'ow' is pronounced differently in 'how' & 'show' **Recognise and use alternative ways of spelling the phonemes already taught,** for example 'ae' can be spelt with 'ai', 'ay' or 'a-e'; begin to know which words contain which spelling alternatives **Identify the constituent parts of two-syllable and three-syllable words** to support the application of phonic knowledge and skills Recognise automatically an increasing number of familiar high frequency words Apply phonic knowledge & skills as the prime approach to reading & spelling unfamiliar words that are not completely decodable **Read more challenging texts** which can be decoded using their acquired phonic knowledge & skills; automatic recognition of high frequency words Read and spell phonically decodable two-syllable and three-syllable words	**Year 1** **Spell new words** using phonics as the prime approach Segment sounds into their constituent phonemes in order to spell them correctly Children **move from spelling simple CVC words to longer words** that include common diagraphs & adjacent consonants such as 'brush', 'crunch' **Recognise & use alternative ways of spelling the graphemes already taught,** for example that the /ae/ sound can be spelt with 'ai', 'ay' or 'a-e'; that the /ee/ sound can also be spelt as 'ea' and 'e'; & begin to know which words contain which spelling alternatives **Use knowledge of common inflections in spelling,** such as plurals, -ly, -er **Read & spell phonically**	**Year 1** **Identify the main events and characters in stories,** and find specific information in simple texts Use syntax and context when reading for meaning **Make predictions** showing an understanding of ideas, events and characters **Recognise the main elements that shape different texts** **Explore the effect of patterns of language &** repeated words & phrases	**Year 1** Select books for personal reading and give reasons for choices **Visualise and comment on events, characters and ideas,** making imaginative links to their own experiences **Distinguish fiction and non-fiction texts and** the different purposes for reading them	**Year 1** **Independently choose what to write about,** plan and follow it through Use key features of narrative in their own writing Convey information and ideas in simple non-narrative forms **Find and use new and interesting words and phrases,** including story language **Create short simple texts on paper and on screen that** combine words with images (and sounds)	**Year 1** Write chronological and non-chronological texts using simple structures **Group written sentences together in chunks** of meaning or subject	**Year 1** **Compose and write simple sentences independently** to communicate meaning **Use capital letters and full stops when** punctuating simple sentences	**Year 1** Write most letters, correctly formed and orientated, using a comfortable and efficient pencil grip Write with spaces between words accurately Use the space bar and keyboard to type their name & simple texts
Year 2 Speak with clarity and use appropriate intonation when reading and reciting texts **Tell real and imagined stories** using the conventions of familiar story language **Explain ideas and processes** using imaginative and adventurous vocabulary and non-verbal gestures to support communication	**Year 2** Listen to others in class, ask relevant questions and follow instructions Listen to talk by an adult, remember some specific points and identify what they have learned **Respond to presentations** by describing characters, repeating some highlight and commenting constructively	**Year 2** **Ensure that everyone contributes,** allocate tasks, and consider alternatives and reach agreement **Work effectively in groups** by ensuring that each group member takes a turn challenging, supporting and moving on Listen to each other's views and preferences, agree the next steps to take and identify contributions by each group member	**Year 2** Adopt appropriate roles in small or large groups and consider alternative courses of action Present part of traditional stories, their own stories or work drawn from different parts of the curriculum for members of their own class **Consider how mood and atmosphere are created** in live or recorded performance	**Year 2** Read independently and with increasing fluency longer and less familiar texts **Spell with increasing accuracy and confidence,** drawing on word recognition and knowledge of word structure, and spelling patterns **Know how to tackle unfamiliar words** that are not completely decodable **Read and spell less common alternative graphemes** including trigraphs **Read high and medium frequency words** independently and automatically	**Year 2** **Spell with increasing accuracy** and confidence, drawing on word recognition and knowledge of word structure, and spelling patterns including common inflections and use of double letters Read and spell less common alternative graphemes including trigraphs **Understanding and interpreting texts**	**Year 2** Draw together ideas & information from across a whole text, using simple signposts in the text **Give reasons why things happen or characters change** Explain organisational features of texts, including alphabetical order, layout, diagrams etc **Use syntax & context** to build their store of vocabulary when reading Explore how particular words are used, including words & expressions with similar meanings	**Year 2** **Read whole books on their own,** choosing and justifying selections Engage with books through exploring and enacting interpretations **Explain their reactions to texts,** commenting on important aspects	**Year 2** Draw on knowledge and experience of texts in deciding and planning what & how to write **Sustain form in narrative,** including use of person & time Maintain consistency in non-narrative, including purpose & tense Make adventurous word and language choices appropriate to the style and purpose of the text **Select from different presentational features to** suit particular writing purposes on paper & on screen	**Year 2** Use planning to establish clear sections for writing Use appropriate language to make sections hang together	**Year 2** Write simple and compound sentences and begin to use subordination in relation to time and reason **Compose sentences using tense consistently** (present & past) Use question marks, and use commas to separate items in a list	**Year 2** Write legibly, using upper and lower case letters appropriately within words, and observing correct spacing within and between words Form and use the four basic handwriting joins **Word process** short narrative and non-narrative texts

NC KS1 Programme of Study - Literacy
(revised framework objectives)

Numeracy 1 using and applying mathematics	Numeracy 2 counting & understanding number	Numeracy 3 knowing & using number	Numeracy 4 calculating	Numeracy 5 understanding shape	Numeracy 6 measuring	Numeracy 7 handling data
Year 1 **Solve problems** involving counting, adding, subtracting, doubling or halving in the context of numbers, measures or money, for example to 'pay' & 'give change' **Describe a puzzle or problem** using numbers, practical materials & diagrams; use these to solve the problem & set the solution in the original context **Answer a question** by selecting and using suitable equipment, and sorting information, shapes or objects; display results using tables and pictures **Describe simple patterns** and relationships involving numbers or shapes; decide whether examples satisfy given conditions **Describe ways of solving puzzles** and problems, explaining choices and decisions orally or using pictures	**Year 1** **Count reliably** at least 20 objects, recognising that when rearranged the number of objects stays the same; estimate a number of objects that can be checked by counting **Compare and order numbers,** using the related vocabulary; use the equals (=) sign **Read and write numerals from 0 to 20,** then beyond; use knowledge of place value to position these numbers on a number track and number line **Say the number that is 1 more or less than any given number,** & 10 more or less for multiples of 10 **Use the vocabulary of halves and quarters** in context	**Year 1** **Derive and recall all pairs of numbers with a total of 10** and addition facts for totals to at least 5; work out the corresponding subtraction facts **Count on or back in ones, twos, fives and tens** and use this knowledge to derive the multiples of 2, 5 and 10 to the tenth multiple **Recall the doubles of all numbers to at least 10**	**Year 1** **Relate addition to counting on;** recognise that addition can be done in any order; use practical and informal written methods to support the addition of a one-digit number or a multiple of 10 to a one-digit or two-digit number **Understand subtraction as 'take away'** and find a 'difference' by counting up; use practical and informal written methods to support the subtraction of a one-digit number from a one-digit or two-digit number and a multiple of 10 from a two-digit number **Use the vocabulary related to addition and subtraction and symbols** to describe and record addition and subtraction number sentences **Solve practical problems** that involve combining groups of 2, 5 or 10, or sharing into equal groups	**Year 1** **Visualise and name common 2-D shapes and 3-D solids** and describe their features; use them to make patterns, pictures & models **Identify objects that turn about a point** (e.g. scissors) or about a line (e.g. a door); recognise & make whole, half & quarter turns **Visualise & use everyday language to describe** the position of objects and direction and distance when moving them, for example when placing or moving objects on a game board	**Year 1** **Estimate, measure, weigh and compare objects,** choosing & using suitable uniform non-standard or standard units & measuring instruments (e.g. a lever balance, metre stick or measuring jug) **Use vocabulary related to time;** order days of the week & months; read the time to the hour & half hour	**Year 1** **Answer a question** by recording information in lists & tables; present outcomes using practical resources, pictures, block graphs or pictograms **Use diagrams to sort objects into groups** according to a given criterion; suggest a different criterion for grouping the same objects
Year 2 **Solve problems** involving addition, subtraction, multiplication or division in contexts of numbers, measures or pounds and pence **Identify and record the information or calculation needed to solve a puzzle or problem**; carry out the steps or calculations and check the solution in the context of the problem **Follow a line of enquiry;** answer questions by choosing and using suitable equipment and selecting, organising and presenting information in lists, tables and simple diagrams **Describe patterns and relationships** involving numbers or shapes, make predictions and test these with examples **Present solutions to puzzles and problems** in an organised way; explain decisions, methods and results in pictorial, spoken or written form, using mathematical language and number sentences	**Year 2** **Read and write two-digit and three-digit numbers in figures and words;** describe and extend number sequences and recognise odd and even numbers **Count up to 100 objects by grouping them and counting in tens, fives or twos;** explain what each digit in a two-digit number represents, including numbers where 0 is a place holder; partition two-digit numbers in different ways, including into multiples of 10 and 1 **Order two-digit numbers** and position them on a number line; use the greater than (>) and less than (<) signs **Estimate a number of objects;** round two-digit numbers to the nearest 10 **Find one half, one quarter and three quarters** of shapes and sets of objects	**Year 2** **Derive and recall all addition and subtraction facts for each number to at least 10,** all pairs with totals to 20 and all pairs of multiples of 10 with totals up to 100 **Understand that halving is the inverse of doubling** and derive and recall doubles of all numbers to 20, and the corresponding halves **Derive and recall multiplication facts for the 2, 5 and 10 times-tables** and the related division facts; recognise multiples of 2, 5 and 10 **Use knowledge of number facts and operations** to estimate and check answers to calculations	**Year 2** **Add or subtract mentally a one-digit number or a multiple of 10 to or from any two-digit number;** use practical and informal written methods to add and subtract two-digit numbers **Understand that subtraction is the inverse of addition and vice versa;** use this to derive and record related addition and subtraction number sentences **Represent repeated addition and arrays as multiplication,** and sharing and repeated subtraction (grouping) as division; use practical and informal written methods and related vocabulary to support multiplication and division, including calculations with remainders **Use the symbols +, −, ?, ÷ and = to record and interpret number sentences** involving all four operations; calculate the value of an unknown in a number sentence	**Year 2** **Visualise common 2-D shapes and 3-D solids;** identify shapes from pictures of them in different positions and orientations; sort, make and describe shapes, referring to their properties **Identify reflective symmetry in patterns and 2-D shapes** and draw lines of symmetry in shapes **Follow and give instructions involving position, direction and movement** **Recognise and use whole, half and quarter turns,** both clockwise and anticlockwise; know that a right angle represents a quarter turn	**Year 2** **Estimate, compare & measure lengths, weights and capacities,** choosing & using standard units (m, cm, kg, litre) & suitable measuring instruments **Read the numbered divisions on a scale,** and interpret the divisions between them (e.g. on a scale from 0 to 25 with intervals of 1 shown but only the divisions 0, 5, 10, 15 and 20 numbered); use a ruler to draw and measure lines to the nearest centimetre **Use units of time (seconds, minutes, hours, days)** and know the relationships between them; read the time to the quarter hour; identify time intervals, including those that cross the hour	**Year 2** **Answer a question by collecting and recording data in lists and tables;** represent the data as block graphs or pictograms to show results; use ICT to organise and present data **Use lists, tables and diagrams to sort objects;** explain choices using appropriate language, including 'not'

Programme of Study - Numeracy (revised framework objectives)

SC1 scientific enquiry			SC2 life processes & living things					SC3 materials and their properties		SC4 physical processes		
Sc1.1 planning	Sc1.2 ideas & evidence; col- lecting evidence	Sc1.3 comparing evidence	Sc2.1 life processes	Sc2.2 humans and other animals	Sc2.3 green plants	Sc2.4 variation and classification	Sc2.5 living things in their environment	Sc3.1 grouping materials	Sc3.2 changing materials	Sc4.1 electricity	Sc4.2 forces and motion	Sc4.3 light and sound
1.1a ask questions 'How?', 'Why?', 'What if'?) and decide how they might find answers to them	1.2a follow simple instructions to control the risks to themselves and to others	1.3a make simple compar- isons (eg, hand span, shoe size) and identify simple patterns or associations, and try to explain it, drawing on their knowledge and understanding	2.1a differences between things that are living and things that have never been alive	2.2a recognise and compare the main external parts of the bodies of humans and other animals	2.3a recognise that plants need light and water to grow	2.4a recognise similar- ities and differ- ences between themselves and others, and to treat others with sensitivity	2.5a find out about the different kinds of plants and animals in the local envi- ronment	3.1a use their senses to explore and recog- nise the similarities and differences between materials	3.2a find out how the shapes of objects made from some materials can be changes by some processes, including squashing, bending, twisting & stretching	4.1a about every- day appli- ances that use electricity	4.2a find out about, & describe the movement of, familiar things (e.g. cars going faster, slowing down, changing direction)	4.3a identify different light sources, including the Sun
1.1b use first-hand experience & simple informa- tion sources to answer ques- tions	1.2b explore, using the senses of sight, hearing, smell, touch & taste as appropriate, & make & record observations & measurements	1.3b compare what hap- pened with what they expected would hap- pen, and try to explain it. Drawing on their knowledge and under- standing	2.1b that animals, including humans, move, feed, grow, use their senses and reproduce	2.2b that humans and other animals need food and water to stay alive	2.3b to recognise and name the leaf, flowers, stem and root of flow- ering plants	2.4b group living things according to observable similarities and differences	2.5b identify similari- ties & differences between local environments & ways in which these affect ani- mals & plants that are found there	3.1b sort objects into groups on the basis of their properties texture, float, hard- ness, transparency & whether they are magnetic or non- magnetic)	3.2b explore & describe the way some everyday materials) for example water, chocolate, bread, clay, change when they are heated or cooled	4.1b simple series circuits involv- ing batteries, wires, bulbs and other components - eg buzzers	4.2b that both pushes and pulls are examples of forces	4.3b that darkness is the absence of light
1.1c think about what might hap- pen before deciding what to do	1.2c communicate what happened in a variety of ways, including using ICT	1.3c review their work and explain what they did to others	2.1c relate life process- es to animals and plants found in the local environ- ment	2.2c that taking exer- cise and eating the right types and amounts of food help humans to keep healthy	2.3c that seeds grow into flowering plants		2.5c care for the envi- ronment	3.1c recognise and name common types of material & recognise that some of them are found naturally		4.1c how a switch can be used to break a cir- cuit	4.2c to recognise that when things speed up, slow down or change direction, there is a cause	4.3c that there are many kinds of sound and sources of sound
1.1d Recognise when a test or comparison is unfair				2.2d about the role of drugs as medi- cines				3.1d find out about the uses of a variety of materials & how these are cho- sen for specific uses on the basis of their simple properties				4.3d that sounds travel away from sources, getting fainter as they do so, and that they are heard

2.2e
how to treat animals with care and sensitivity

2.2f
that humans and other animals can produce offspring and that these offspring grow into adults

2.2g
about the senses that enable humans and other
animals to be aware of the world around them

NC KS1 Programme of Study for Key Stage 1 - Science

NC KS1 Programme of Study - ICT

ICT 1 — 1.1 finding things out / 1.2 developing ideas and making things happen		ICT 2 exchanging and sharing information	ICT 3 reviewing, modifying & evaluating work as it progresses	ICT 4 breadth of study
1.1a gather information from a variety of sources	1.2a use text, tables, images & sound to develop their ideas	2a share their ideas by presenting information in a variety of forms	3a review what they have done to help them develop their ideas	4a work with a range of information to investigate the ways it can be presented
1.1b enter & store information in a variety of forms	1.2b select from and add to information they have	2b present their completed work effectively	3b describe the effects of their actions	4b exploring a variety of ICT tools
1.1c retrieve information that has been stored	1.2c plan & give instructions to make things happen		3c talk about what they might change in future work	4c talk about the uses of ICT inside and outside school
	1.2d try things out & explore what happens in real & imaginary instructions			

NC KS1 Programme of Study - History

H1 chronological understanding	H2 K & U of events, people &changes	H3 historical interpretation	H4 historical enquiry	H5 organisation & communication	H6 breadth of study
1a place events and objects in chronological order	2a recognise why people did things, why events happened and what happened as a result	3a identify different ways in which the past is represented	4a find out about the past from a range of sources of information	5a select from their knowledge of history and communicate it in a variety of ways	6a changes in their own lives and the way of life of their family or others around them
1b use common words and phrases relating to the passing of time (for example, before, after, a long time ago, past	2b identify differences between ways of life at different times		4b ask and answer questions about the past		6b the way of life of people in the more distant past who lived in the local area or elsewhere in Britain
					6c the lives of significant men, women and children
					6d past events from the history of Britain and the wider world

NC KS1 Programme of Study - D&T

D&T 1 developing planning & communicating ideas	D&T 2 working with tools, equipment, materials	D&T 3 evaluating processes & products	D&T 4 k & u of materials & components	D&T 5 breadth of study
1a generate ideas	2a explore sensory qualities of materials	3a talk about their ideas	4a working characteristics of materials	5a focused practical tasks
1b develop ideas	2b measure, mark out, cut and shape	3b identify improvements	4b how mechanisms can be used	5b design & make assignments
1c talk about their ideas	2c assemble, join & combine materials			5c investigate & evaluate products
1d plan what to do next	2d use simple finishing techniques			
1e communicate ideas	2e follow safe procedures			

NC KS1 Programme of Study - Geography

G1.1 & G1.2 geographical and enquiry skills		G2 knowledge & understanding of places	G3 knowledge & understanding of patterns & processes	G4 knowledge & understanding of environment	G5 breadth of study
1.1a ask geographical questions	1.2a use geographical vocabulary	2a identify & describe what places are like	3a make observations about where things are located	4a recognise changes in the environment	5a the locality of the school
1.1b observe and record	1.2b use fieldwork skills	2b identify and describe what places are	3b recognise changes in physical & human features	4b recognise how the environment may be improved & sustained	5b a contrasting locality in the UK or overseas
1.1c express their own views about people, places & environments	1.2c use globes, maps & plans at a range of scales	2c recognise how places become they way they are & how they are changing			5c study at a local scale
1.1d communicate in different ways	1.2d use secondary sources of information	2d recognise how places compare with other places			5d carry out fieldwork investigations outside the classroom
		2e recognise how places are linked to other places in the world			

Programme of Study for Key Stage 1 - Art & Design

A&D1 exploring & developing ideas	A&D2 investigating & making art, craft and design	A&D3 evaluating & developing work	A&D4 k & u of materials & components	A&D5 breadth of study
1a record from first hand observation, experience & imagination	2a investigate the possibilities of materials and processes	3a review what they and others have done	4a visual and tactile elements	5a exploring a range of starting points
1b ask and answer questions about the starting points for their work	2b try out tools & techniques & apply these	3b identify what they might change	4b materials & processes used in making art, craft & design	5b working on their own, and collaborating with others
	2c represent observations, ideas and feelings		4c differences & similarities in the work of artists, craftspeople & designers	5c using a range of materials and processes
				5d investigating different kinds of art, craft & design

Programme of Study for Key Stage 1 - Music

M1 performing skills	M2 composing skills	M3 responding & reviewing (appraising skills)	M4 responding & reviewing (listening skills)	M5 breadth of study
1a use their voices expressively by singing songs, chants, rhymes	2a create musical patterns	3a explore and express their ideas and feelings about music	4a listen with concentration & internalise & recall sounds	5a a range of musical activities
1b play tuned & untuned instruments	2b explore, choose & organise sounds & musical ideas	3b make improvements to their own work	4b how combined musical elements can be organised	5b responding to a range of starting points
1c rehearse and perform with others			4c how sounds can be made in different ways	5c working on their own, in groups & as a class
				5d a range of live and recorded music

Programme of Study for Key Stage 1 - PE

PE1 acquiring and developing skills	PE2 selecting and applying skills, tactics and compositional ideas	PE3 evaluating and improving performance	PE4 knowledge and understanding of fitness and health	PE5 breadth of study
1a explore basic skills, actions and ideas with increasing understanding	2a explore how to choose & apply skills and actions in sequence & in combination	3a describe what they have done	4a how important it is to be active	5a dance
1b remember & repeat simple skills & actions with increasing control	2b vary the way they perform skills by using simple tactics and movement phrases	3b observe, describe & copy what others have done	4b recognise & describe how their bodies feel during different activities	5b games
	2c apply rules and conventions for different activities	3c use what they have learnt to improve the quality and control of their work		5c gymnastics

Programme of Study for Key Stage 1 - PSHE

PSHEC1 developing confidence & responsibility & making the most of their abilities	PSHEC2 preparing to play an active role as citizens	PSHEC3 developing a healthier lifestyle	PSHEC4 developing good relationships & respecting differences
1a recognise their likes & dislikes, what is fair & unfair, what is right & wrong	2a take part in discussions with one other person and the whole class	3a make simple choices that improve their health & wellbeing	4a recognise how their behaviour affects other people
1b share their opinions on things that matter to them and their views	2b take part in a simple debate about topical issues	3b maintain personal hygiene	4b listen to other people and play and work co-operatively
1c recognise, name and deal with their feelings in a positive way	2c recognise choices they make, & the difference between right & wrong	3c how some diseases spread and can be controlled	4c identify and respect differences and similarities between people
1d think about themselves, learn from their experiences & recognise what they are good at	2d realise that people and other living things have needs, & that they have responsibilities to meet them	3d about the process of growing from young to old & how people's needs change	4d that family and friends should care for each other
1e how to set simple goals	2e that they belong to various groups & communities, such as a family	3e the names of the main parts of the body	4e that there are different types of teasing & bullying, that bullying is wrong
	2f what improves & harms their local, natural & built environments	3f that household products & medicines, can be harmful	
	2g contribute to the life of the class and school	3g rules for, and ways of, keeping safe, basic road safety	
	2h realise that money comes from different sources		

Credits and references

The following organisations and individuals have kindly given permission for photographs to be used in this book:

The cardboard school building on page 43: CABE/ School of Architecture & Planning, University of Newcastle www.cabe.org.uk

The Darlington Train in Morrison's car park, page 19: Picture courtesy of David Byers, www.darlington-life.co.uk

Japanese Stones on page 5: www.outlandstone.co.uk sell stones & pebbles in lovely colours, look at the picture, but you have to buy at least 25kg of each or share a bag with someone else!

Tipi Tents page 59: for the photo of a reproduction (but genuine) Native American tipi www.tipi-tents.co.uk

Thanks to East Leeds Early Years Centre and North Tyneside and Merton LAs for photos of their resources and children's work (pages 59, 61, 63, 64, 68)

Web sites included in this book (in alphabetical order):

www.annelyjudafineart.co.uk to look at wrapping works by Christo and Jeanne Claude

www.artastic.co.uk for paper Artstraws and books on how to use them

www.technologysupplies.co.uk for paper Artstraws

www.artcraft.co.uk have a huge range of craft supplies, including sticks; the site also has an index of craft sites across the UK

www.art-tek.co.uk (click through to education/projects) has some good examples of bridges

www.ascoeducational.co.uk for Link Kits (big size), Mobilo, Maxi-Kit Tech.

www.bbc.co.uk/gardening/gardening_with_children for ideas and projects

www.bdp.co.uk/structures/engineering the site of a structural engineering company

www.beadworks.co.uk the on line store of the Bead Shop

www.brick.org.uk or www.archinet.co.uk for brick suppliers

www.brio.co.uk education suppliers

www.buildingcentre.org.uk The Building Centre

www.bushcraftexpeditions.com click through to UK courses/junior courses for photos of stick and camping structures

www.buystone.co.uk/pebbles have lovely pictures on the website and polished stones cheap! they also have really interesting things like fossilised wood

www.cabe.org.uk CABE (the Commission for Architecture and the Built Environment) for photos of new schools and other buildings

www.canestore.co.uk for cane and other craft supplies

www.cleapss.org.uk (Consortium of LAs for the provision of Science Services)

www.cobcottage.com mud walls and cob cottage pictures

www.communityplaythings.co.uk Community Playthings, suppliers of high quality wooden furniture and bricks

www.constructiontoys.com for Erector, Querceti Marble Run and Lincoln Logs - a kit for making model log cabins

www.dandys.org have coloured glass and slate

www.deltasand.com for Delta Sand (mouldable sand)

www.ebay.co.uk crafters section

www.elc.co.uk Early Learning Centre, shop and site for toys and educational resources

www.eduzone.co.uk Eduzone, education supplier

www.englishwillowbaskets.co.uk for basket making supplies and lots of photos of baskets

Coleg Sir Gâr
Canolfan Dysgu
Ammanford
Learning Centre

www.emporiumuk.biz have a massive range of glass beads, marbles and other decorative beads

www.englishwillowbaskets.co.uk for basket making supplies and lots of photos of baskets

www.foresteducation.org.uk Forest Education

www.forestschools.com Forest Schools home website

www.fs.org.uk the Royal Forestry Society, has a strong interest in education projects

www.hazelwattle.com and click on photos for fencing and wattle making

www.naturalfencing.com for living willow and other fencing

www.hope-education.co.uk Hope: education supplier

www.kidscanmakeit.com woodworking activities, tools, tips, ideas for children and books from

ww.ltl.org.uk Learning Through Landscapes

www.leevalley.com has goggles and woodwork tools

www.lego.com the Lego website

www.mailorderexpress.com for Galt products, Connecta-straws and Straw Art Kits

www.newclay.co.uk for self hardening clay

www.organicgardening.org.uk major organic growing website

www.outlandstone.co.uk sell stones and pebbles in lovely colours, look at the pictures, but you have to buy at least 25kg of each or share a bag!

www.paperfolding.com will give you some ideas and diagrams for models

www.recycling-guide.org.uk/activities has recycling guidance for schools and some ideas of simple things to make

www.scrapstore.co.uk and

www.scrapstore.org will give you help in locating scrapstores near your

www.solardome.co.uk has a range of photos of geodesic domes

www.sparkofinspiration.co.uk for construction kits with sticks and balls and magnetic sets

www.strawcraftmen.co.uk the Guild of Straw Craftsmen

www.tarquinbooks.com a site that has lots of books on technology

www.teachernet.gov.uk/management/resourcesfinanceandbuildings/schoolbuildings/exemplars/primary website link to all sorts of government initiatives

www.texere.co.uk Texere Yarns for natural wool, fleece, braids and cords

www.thebeadshop.co.uk more beads and other decorative items

www.thewillowbank.com for a DVD of how to make living willow structures

www.thorlogcabins.co.uk or www.loghomebuilders.org.uk log cabins and how to build them

www.twigpencils.co.uk for all sorts of twig and wood products

www.321toys.co.uk or www.teifoc.com (the home site) for Teifoc miniature brick building sets

www.vvrouleaux.com for all sorts of yarns, braids, beads & other trimmings

www.wealdown.co.uk (the Weald and Downland Museum in Sussex)

www.wikipedia.org to get reference material and picture

www.willowworks.co.uk for living willow projects for schools (see photos)

www.ysp.co.uk Yorkshire Sculpture Park

www.ysp.co.uk/education/projects the site for the Yorkshire Sculpture Park where children can work with natural and found materials

www.foresteducation.org.uk Forest Education
www.forestschools.com Forest Schools home website
www.fs.org.uk the Royal Forestry Society, has a strong interest in education projects
www.hazelwattle.com and click on photos for fencing and wattle making
www.naturalfencing.com for living willow and other fencing
www.hope-education.co.uk Hope: education supplier
www.kidscanmakeit.com woodworking activities, tools, tips, ideas for children and books
ww.ltl.org.uk Learning Through Landscapes
www.leevalley.com has goggles and woodwork tools
www.lego.com the Lego website

www.mailorderexpress.com for Galt products, Connecta-straws and Straw Art Kits
www.newclay.co.uk for self hardening clay
www.organicgardening.org.uk major organic growing website
www.outlandstone.co.uk sell stones and pebbles in lovely colours, look at the pictures, but you have to buy at least 25kg of each or share a bag!
www.paperfolding.com will give you some ideas and diagrams for models
www.recycling-guide.org.uk/activities has recycling guidance for schools and some ideas of simple things to make
www.scrapstore.co.uk and
www.scrapstore.org will give you help in locating scrapstores near your
www.solardome.co.uk has a range of photos of geodesic domes
www.sparkofinspiration.co.uk for construction kits with sticks and balls and magnetic sets
www.strawcraftmen.co.uk the Guild of Straw Craftsmen

www.tarquinbooks.com a site that has lots of books on technology
www.teachernet.gov.uk/management/resourcesfinanceandbuildings/schoolbuildings/exemplars/primary website link to all sorts of government initiatives
www.texere.co.uk Texere Yarns for natural wool, fleece, braids and cords
www.thebeadshop.co.uk more beads and other decorative items
www.thewillowbank.com for a DVD of how to make living willow structures
www.thorlogcabins.co.uk or www.loghomebuilders.org.uk log cabins and how to build them
www.twigpencils.co.uk for all sorts of twig and wood products
www.321toys.co.uk or www.teifoc.com (the home site) for Teifoc miniature brick building sets
www.vvrouleaux.com for all sorts of yarns, braids, beads & other trimmings
www.wealdown.co.uk (the Weald and Downland Museum in Sussex)
www.wikipedia.org to get reference material and picture
Shiam Wilcox (recycled materials artist) can be contacted on shiam@talk21.com
www.willowworks.co.uk for living willow projects for schools (see photos)
www.ysp.co.uk Yorkshire Sculpture Park
www.ysp.co.uk/education/projects the site for the Yorkshire Sculpture Park where children can work with natural and found materials

NB
These websites and addresses are correct at the time of printing. Please let us know if you find other interesting sources or contacts sally@featherstone.uk.com.

Carrying on in Key Stage One

Other titles in this series:

Sand

Water

Role Play

Outdoor Play

Sculpting, stuffing and Squeezing

www.acblack.com/featherstone

The EYFS – Birth to Three

Little Baby Books offer lots of ideas for working with young children, and match the original birth to three framework.

A Strong Child   **A Skilful Communicator**   **A Competent Learner**   **A Healthy Child**

Set 1
978-1-905019-21-2

Set 2
978-1-905019-22-9

Set 3
978-1-905019-23-6

Set 4
978-1-905019-24-3

Also available with the activities grouped according to stage.

Book 1 Heads-up Lookers & Communicators (124pp)
978-1-905019-50-2

Book 2 Sitters, Standers & Explorers (156pp)
978-1-905019-51-9

Book 3 Movers, Shakers & Players (172pp)
978-1-905019-52-6

Book 4 Walkers, Talkers & Pretenders (238pp)
978-1-905019-53-3

All the activities in these books are suitable for the EYFS. Just look for the component and age you need.

Heads-up Lookers & Communicators — Stage 1: 0-8 months

Sitters, Standers & Explorers — Stage 2: 8-18 months

Movers, Shakers & Players — Stage 3: 18-24 months

Walkers, Talkers & Pretenders — Stage 4: 24-36 months

Foundations Activity Packs

Ages 3–5

Each pack: ● pbk, resources & CD **£24.99** ● 305 x 225 mm
● 48pp ● colour photographs, black and white illustrations

WINNER — NLA WOW! AWARD 2004 — era WINNER

These award-winning activity packs are bursting with resources – ideal for all adults working with children aged 3–5.

Written by Early Years practitioners and experts.

"Everything you need to plan, organise and lead activities on early years themes"
Montessori International

The resources in each pack include:

● 50+ easy-to-follow activities
● 14 photocopiable activity sheets
● 8 colour photocards
● CD of poems, songs and stories
● Giant themed display poster
● Planning chart

  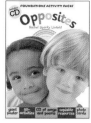

Celebrations
Kate Tucker
9780713668452

Opposites
Rachel Sparks Linfield
9780713662191

My School Day
Ann Montague-Smith
9780713661583

Minibeasts
Christine Moorcroft
9780713662184

Playsongs

 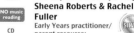

Livelytime Playsongs
Sheena Roberts & Rachel Fuller
Early Years practitioner/ parent resource:
● **£9.99**
● pbk (32pp) + CD
9780713669404

Baby's active day in songs and pictures.
A picture songbook which tells the story of a baby's day in glorious full colour and in songs with clearly described actions. Dances, peekaboo, finger and toeplays, teasers, knee bouncers and lullabies. 0–3 years

Sleepytime Playsongs
Sheena Roberts & Rachel Fuller
Early Years practitioner/ parent resource:
● **£9.99**
● pbk (32pp) + CD
9780713669411

Baby's restful day in songs and pictures.
A picture songbook and CD which tells the story of baby's restful day in glorious full colour and in songs with clearly described actions. 0–3 years

Playsongs
Early Years/practitioner/ parent resource:
● **£12.99**
● pbk (48pp) + CD
9780713663716

72 songs and rhymes for babies and toddlers.
The perfect musical start for the very young – fully illustrated book and CD. 0–3 years

To see our full range of books visit www.acblack.com

Continuity and progression through the EYFS

The Baby & Beyond series takes simple activities or resources and shows how they can be used with children at each of the EYFS development stages, from birth to 60+ months. Each double page spread covers one activity, so you can see the progression at a glance.

Shows how simple resources can be used by children at different ages and stages

Inspiration for planning continuous provision

Ideal to support progression and extend learning.

Messy Play	978-1-905019-58-8
The Natural World	978-1-905019-57-1
The Sensory World	978-1-905019-60-1
Sound and Music	978-1-905019-59-5
Mark Making	978-1-905019-78-6
Construction	978-1-905019-77-9
Dolls & Soft Toys	978-1-905019-80-9
Bikes, Prams, Pushchairs	978-1-905019-76-2
Role Play	978-1-906029-02-9
Finger Play & Rhymes	978-1-906029-01-2
Dens & Shelters	978-1-906029-03-6
Food	978-1-906029-04-3

To see our full range of books visit www.acblack.com